BMW

Classic Cars of the 1960s and 70s

Other Titles in the Crowood AutoClassics Series

AC Cobra	Brian Laban
Alfa Romeo Spider	John Tipler
Aston Martin: DB4, DB5 and DB6	Jonathan Wood
Aston Martin and Lagonda V-Engined Cars	David G Styles
BMW M-Series	Alan Henry
Carbodies	Bill Munro
Citroën 2CV	Matt White
Citroën DS	Jon Pressnell
Datsun Z Series	David G Styles
Ferrari Dino	Anthony Curtis
Jaguar E-Type	Jonathan Wood
Jaguar Mk1 and 2	James Taylor
Jaguar S-Type and 420	James Taylor
Jaguar XJ Series	Graham Robson
Jaguar XJ-S	Graham Robson
Jaguar XK Series	Jeremy Boyce
Lamborghini Countach	Peter Dron
Land-Rover	John Tipler
Lotus and Caterham Seven: Racers for the Road	John Tipler
Lotus Elan	Mike Taylor
Lotus Esprit	Jeremy Walton
Mercedes SL Series	Brian Laban
MGA	David G Styles
MGB	Brian Laban
MG T-Series	Graham Robson
Mini	James Ruppert
Morris Minor	Ray Newell
Porsche 356	David G Styles
Porsche 911	David Vivian
Porsche 924/928/944/968	David Vivian
Range Rover	James Taylor and Nick Dimbleby
Rolls-Royce Silver Shadow	Graham Robson
Rover P4	James Taylor
Rover P5 and P5B	James Taylor
Rover SD1	Karen Pender
Sprites and Midgets	Anders Ditlev Clausager
Sunbeam Alpine and Tiger	Graham Robson
Triumph TRs	Graham Robson
Triumph 2000 and 2.5PI	Graham Robson
TVR	John Tipler
VW Beetle	Robert Davies
VW Transporter	Laurence Meredith

BMW

The Classic Cars of the 1960s and 70s

Laurence Meredith

First published in 1999 by
The Crowood Press Ltd
Ramsbury, Marlborough
Wiltshire SN8 2HR

British Library Cataloguing-in-Publication Data
A catalogue record for this book is available from the
British Library.

ISBN 1 86126 250 7

Acknowledgements
The author is grateful to the following: Mark Garfitt,
Jill Watson, John Day, BMW, Dr Ralph Schmidt,
Gill Boase, Tony Halse (Munich Legends), Kevin Lane,
Martin Trainer, Graham J. Arnold, James Booth,
Paul Silcox, Philip Porter and Hans-Joachim Stuck.

Typeset by Florence Production Ltd, Stoodleigh, Devon
Printed and bound in Great Britain by The Bath Press

Contents

BMW Evolution

1928   BMW builds its first car: the Dixi, an Austin 7 copy made under licence from the British manufacturer. The small car is reasonably successful throughout the years of global economic recession ahead.

1929   The Dixi is developed and relies less and less on components imported from Britain. The famous BMW badge appears on the radiator shell from the beginning of the year.

1932   After just four years the Dixi is discontinued, being replaced by the 3/20. This was arguably the first true BMW car, and boasted independent suspension at all four wheels.

1934   The first BMW sports car is launched and dubbed the 315/1 Sports. With its 1.5-litre in-line 6-cylinder engine, the car was capable of well in excess of 70mph (110km/h). The 1.9-litre 319/1 Sport that followed would be regarded as one of the great cars of the 1930s. In this same year the Aldington brothers are so impressed by the performance of the works 315/1s on the Alpine Rally that they import BMWs to Britain and market them as Frazer Nash BMWs.

1936   Ernst Henne takes a BMW 328 to victory at the Nürburgring at an average speed of 63mph (101km/h). This was a stunning debut for the new car, which would go into production shortly after. A truly great machine, the 328 would influence the styling of the Jaguar XK120 debuted in 1948.

1940   A special coupe version of the 328 is driven to outright victory on the Mille Miglia by Huschke von Hanstein and Walter Baumer. Their average speed for this tough event was a blistering 104mph (166km/h).

1941   Car production is halted for the duration of the War.

1949   A small motorcycle-powered car is designed but fails to reach production.

1951   BMW enters the luxury saloon market and displays the 501 at the Frankfurt Auto Show. The era of 'Baroque Angels' has begun.

1954   A revised 501A debuts, and a 2.6-litre V8 appears at the Geneva Motor Show, but these cars were always expensive and eventually bowed out in 1963.

1955   The 507 sports car is shown at the Frankfurt Show, and warmly applauded for its beautiful styling and advanced performance. In the same year the Isetta 'bubble' car was launched, and allowed the company to ride the storm produced by the Suez crisis.

1959   A large injection of money from the Quandt family rescues BMW from almost certain bankruptcy, and allows the company to develop a new, more modern car.

1961   The 1500 saloon is exhibited at the Frankfurt Auto Show; a good looking three-box saloon with fine handling and exemplary performance, this car revives BMW's flagging fortunes.

1963   Work begins on the development of the 1800 and 2-litre models, the latter appearing in 1966 with rectangular headlamps. Both are a huge success and allow for the development of further models.

1965   Styled 'in-house', the 2-door 2000CS pillarless coupe debuts and, despite controversial aesthetics, re-establishes BMW's reputation as a maker of luxury sporting machinery.

1966   Launch of the 2-door 1600-02 broadens the appeal of the BMW range and sets new standards among lightweight, mid-range saloons.

1968   The debut of the 4-cylinder 2002 and a new range of 6-cylinder coupés and saloons sets BMW on the road to 'super stardom' in the manufacture of high quality sporting machinery.

1971   A 3-door Touring, or estate, version of the '02 series goes into production, and pre-dates Volkswagen's Golf GTi 'hot hatch' by some five years.

1972   The all new 5 Series is launched, at first with a 2-litre 4-cylinder engine, and from the following year with a 2.5-litre 'six'. With development, this model would be hailed in many quarters as the world's best all-round sporting saloon.

1973   BMW's talent for innovative engineering results in the development of the world's first production turbocharged car - the 2002 turbo. Fast but thirsty, this model is dropped in 1974 due to the Middle East oil crisis after the production of just 1,672 examples.

1976   A watershed year in which the 2002 and 3.0CS coupes are replaced by the 3 Series and 6 Series respectively.

1977   The big, luxurious 7 Series joins the range, and seriously threatens Daimler-Benz's supreme position as a manufacturer of luxury Grand Tourers.

1981   The 5 Series is redesigned and becomes one of Europe's most sought-after cars.

1983   Nelson Piquet wins the Formula One Championship in a Brabham BT52 powered by a turbocharged 1.5-litre BMW engine.

1995   A V12 BMW engine powers a McLaren F1 to outright victory at Le Mans.

1999   An open-top BMW Spyder takes victory at Le Mans after benefiting from the misfortunes of others, and provides further impetus for the development of a new Grand Prix engine for use during the 2000 season.

Introduction

GLOOM TO BOOM

The BMW story is almost, but not quite, unfathomable. From the early days as a successful aero-engine manufacturer, through the doom and economic gloom of the post-War years, to the quite extraordinary success of today, the intrigue that lies behind the Bavarian engineering supremo is not only compelling from a historical point of view, but considerably stranger than fiction.

The rise, fall and rise again of the Bavarian Motor Works could have only happened in Germany, where long-term investment in both people and production, coupled with hard work, is a long tried, tested and proven formula for economic success. These facets are all part of German national character and one reason why BMW, after being brought to the brink of financial disaster in 1959, is one of the automotive world's greatest and cleverest success stories.

THE BUBBLE BURSTS

During the late 1950s and early 1960s, there were few who aspired to BMW ownership as they do today. In an attempt to save its post-1956 Suez crisis bacon, BMW took to manufacturing inexpensive 'microcars'. These were strange devices that, on the one hand provided basic, economical transport, but on the other proved to be about as useful as a French dictionary in an Australian restaurant when it came to loading up the

Despite the passing of 80 years, it's still difficult to believe that BMW's meteoric rise to success started in the late 1920s with a car based on the humble Austin 7.

Pre-war masterpiece, the BMW 328 (seen here at Prescott in Ken McMaster's hands) launched BMW's reputation as a builder of some of the world's finest sports cars.

One of the best handling sports saloons of the late 1960s, the 2002 provided a rock-solid base for further development. Now rightly regarded as a classic design, the 2002 remains a firm favourite among BMW aficionados.

family for an annual holiday. 'Bubble' cars had their place, of course, and served their purpose well enough, but hardly constituted the 'ultimate driving experience'.

Today, the company is at the forefront of research into the use of hydrogen as an alternative to fossil fuels, is heavily involved in designing a new engine for Formula One racing (possibly with a view to reviving the fortunes of the flagging Williams Grand Prix concern), and produces some of the very best road cars.

It's a moot point, but BMW constantly challenges, and often wins the battle against Daimler-Benz for the coveted and unofficial title of the manufacturer of the 'World's Best Car'. So good are the vehicles from both German manufacturers, that this little wrangle is purely subjective and largely academic, although it remains to be seen what fruit is borne from the Bavarian company's purchase of the right to use the Rolls-Royce name.

Between the start of the 1950s, when the company was producing stolid, luxury saloons that were too expensive to be afforded by a nation recovering from the ravages of the Second World War, through the real possibility of bankruptcy in the latter part of that decade and huge success today, the company has undergone transition from rags to riches like no other motor manufacturer.

Here in Britain we are well used to stories about motor manufacturing disappointments and disasters, but the reasons behind these are very different from BMW's past misfortunes. The sad yarn of the British Motor Corporation (later British Leyland, BL and now the Rover Group), is largely one of complacency, ineptitude and successive ranges of outdated motor cars that few outside Britain wanted to buy.

Japanese investment went a long way towards rescuing large chunks of the British motor industry; BMW has also made important input by taking over the running and ownership of the Rover group. In 1998 there were signs that the Bavarian giant has cause to regret getting involved. That BMW have come such a long way is not, *per se*, particularly astonishing. But its meteoric rise in such a short period – the same period that has seen the death of so many manufacturers – is almost incredible.

BADGE 'HYPE'

Many believe this success to be largely the result of clever marketing. This is not wholly true, although strong marketing has certainly played a part in how BMW's products are perceived globally. I have been told on numerous occasions that BMW owners pay handsomely for a bonnet badge – the same style badge that once sat proudly on the front panel of the company's 'bubble' cars.

Down the years I have driven many BMWs of all breeds and tried, difficult as it has sometimes been, to be objective when writing about them for assorted motoring journals. It falls to the lot of motoring journalists to test all manner of motor cars – a hazard of the job – and I drew the conclusion a long time ago that BMW's standards are the equal of their two major rivals in Stuttgart, namely Daimler-Benz and Porsche. Naturally, it's a personal choice, but I happen to prefer BMW styling, which is why I own and drive a Bavarian product. And my decision to part with hard-earned cash for one of these fine machines certainly wasn't based on the allure of an 'overpriced' bonnet badge.

In recent times the famous motif – the blue and white of Bavaria's state colours and 'frozen' aeroplane propeller design – has come to symbolize the very essence of engineering integrity and excellence. This perception is not based on claims made by BMW's clever marketing and advertising people, but on what a BMW feels like from the driver's seat, and on its ability to travel many thousands of miles without requiring major and expensive mechanical surgery.

But BMWs are expensive, aren't they? Go to the factory and see how they're made, and it's not difficult to appreciate why these magnificent cars cost a little, or a lot more, than the products of some rival manufacturers. In all aspects of design – styling, performance, safety, fuel consumption and innovation – the designers and engineers in Munich endeavour, and usually succeed, in staying one or two steps ahead of the opposition.

It wasn't a coincidence that Grand Prix car designer Gordon Murray selected the mighty BMW V12 engine and gearbox from the 8-series to power the McLaren F1, one of the world's fastest 'supercars'. There were many other power units that this South African genius might have chosen for this ambitious programme, but few, if any, produced the formidable horsepower figures required. In 1995 a BMW-powered McLaren F1 won the Le Mans 24 Hours, which at least went some way to silencing ill-informed criticism that BMWs were little more than a 'hyped-up' marketing man's dream.

Naturally, a car built specially for Le Mans is far removed from our everyday roadgoing machinery. At BMW, though, engineering targets are always the same – to manufacture to the highest possible standards. But, for the time being, ignore BMW's strength in the fields of primary and secondary safety, first-class roadholding and all the other points for which the road cars are renowned, there is one enduring trait of the company's products that endears them to people, who enjoy the art and science of driving for their own sake.

THE RIGHT WAY FORWARDS

That trait is that BMWs – all BMWs – continue to be made with rear-wheel drive, and it is this above all else, that sets BMW, and other serious car manufacturers, above and away from the herd. It is easy to understand why other car makers have taken the front-wheel drive route. It is cheaper, eases the lot of production engineers, and promotes handling characteristics which are arguably safer in unskilled or inexperienced hands.

To compensate for its inherent deficiencies – understeer, torquesteer and wheelspin – manufacturers have been forced to employ ever-wider soft compound tyres, wider front and rear track and, in many cases, electronic traction control devices.

By the late 1960s BMW had well and truly set its sights on conquering Daimler-Benz's supremacy in the luxury saloon market.

Some companies have overcome these usual front-drive problems with advanced chassis engineering – a triumph of engineering over design – and cars like the Golf GTi and Saab turbos work well enough, even at the limit. But for experienced drivers of 'proper' cars (and purists alike), there's no getting away from rear-wheel drive, whether or not the engine is situated in front of, or behind, the driver.

As a teenager in the early 1970s who spent almost every waking hour thinking about the world's most exciting cars, BMWs made a huge impression on me. Family holidays comprised long sojourns to Italy, taking in the French motorway network *en route*. In August every year the Route Nationale running from Paris to the south was both a terrifying and exciting place. August is a time when the French, Dutch, Scandinavians, Germans and British take holidays in their thousands, and all without exception are impatient to reach the sun-soaked beaches and sweltering discos of the French and Italian Rivieras.

During our 1973 annual trip the family Volvo 145S estate car sat firmly in the middle lane of the motorway – all three lanes were running virtually bumper-to-bumper. The outside lane was filled with the quickest and fastest cars. There were the big 'Bee-ems', Mercs, Citroën-Maseratis, Renault Alpines and the occasional Ferrari Dino 246 or 365 GTB 'Daytona'. They were all going like stink, and I urged my late father to join in with the 'race'. He refused out of a sense of self-preservation and also explained that, as the top speed of the Volvo was limited to 105mph, we would incur the wrath of following traffic by getting in the way.

As the metallic silver of the 'Silver Arrows' from Stuttgart and Munich flashed by in the unbearable heat of the day, I resolved as a 15-year-old that one day I would own a BMW.

With the beautiful 3.0CS Coupé, the clever people in Munich had not only prodded Daimler-Benz into action, but had also given Porsche food for serious thought.

GOLDEN ERA

This book covers a long period of BMW history. From pioneering days to the present, all BMWs are important, but the classic cars of the 1960s and 1970s are by far and away the most exciting, because they were built during the company's most challenging and difficult times. From the beautifully devised 1500 saloon that made its debut in 1961 to the last of the CS coupés of the mid-1970s, these cars came at a time of steep learning for BMW. They not only made a huge impression on schoolboys like me, but on two generations, and more, of sporting enthusiasts. It was also a period in which BMW established itself as a company to be reckoned with: Daimler-Benz, Jaguar and Alfa-Romeo would ignore the people in southern Germany at their peril.

Many of the models made during this era are acknowledged classics, and much sought after by collectors. Cars like the 2002, which set new standards of road-holding for mid-range saloons in the mid-1960s, are correctly regarded as legends. Properly restored or original examples command premium prices today.

Interestingly, the late Denis Jenkinson, doyen of motoring journalists and Continental correspondent of the revered British journal *Motor Sport*, was once asked to compile a list of his top ten favourite motor cars. 'Jenks', as he was affectionately known, spent virtually all his adult life with interesting cars, competed widely in a variety of sporting competitions and simply lived for motor cars. He drove every important vehicle of his day, reporting on each for *Motor Sport* in his inimitable style. He was famous and respected for holding strong opinions – you always knew where you were with Jenks. For example, he refused to drive the VW-Porsche 914 when it was launched in 1969.

He considered the styling to be ridiculous and commented that it was difficult to tell whether this mid-engined machine was coming or going. However, he held the BMW 2002 in such high regard that it was included in his top ten of all-time greats for its superlative road manners, and ability to run rings around cars with appreciably more engine power.

During the 'classic' and heady period covered in this volume, BMW came to the forefront as world-class innovators. The Karmann-built bodies for the CS coupés, for example, are acknowledged as being among the best-looking sports saloon styles ever, and their 6-cylinder engines the smoothest. BMW's famous claim that a coin could be placed vertically on the 'cambox' of their 6-cylinder engine, and not topple over with the motor running at tickover, was not an extravagant one.

Technical innovation at BMW led to the world's first production turbocharged car – the 2002 turbo – but, unfortunately, this fabulously quick little machine fell victim to the 1973 Middle East oil crisis.

In 1973 BMW introduced the world's first production turbo-engined car, and although this version of the 2002 was shortlived because of the fuel crisis in the Middle East, it pointed the way forwards for other manufacturers, particularly in the controversial field of diesel engine technology.

During 1972 and 1973 when international sports car racing was going through one of its periodic dull phases, BMW brought the racetracks back to life with the totally outrageous 'Batmobile' coupés. When these were pitted against the powerful Cologne-built Ford Capris, some of the twentieth-century's finest motoring track battles were fought. BMW usually came out on top, particularly when the German ace, Hans Joachim-Stuck was at the wheel.

Success in motor racing continued long after the production demise of these fabulous cars, the highlight being Nelson Piquet's victory in the 1983 Formula One Driver's Championship with the 1.5-litre turbocharged BMW-engined Brabham. This, though, is another fantastic BMW story and beyond the scope of this book. More important at this stage is the company's history, which is essential to delve into first, not only because it is interesting, but because the more turbulent periods laid the very foundations on which the firm's success is based today.

THE CRITICS

During the course of writing this book, I have tried to convey my enthusiasm for the BMW marque, and it necessarily follows that much of it is of a highly subjective nature. For this I make no apologies. Naturally, I have selectively quoted the views of contemporary writers who described the cars when they were new, but

A feat of advanced engineering refinement, the 750i V12 of the modern era is among the world's best ever cars. Its vastly powerful engine contributed to McLaren's victory in the Le Mans 24-Hours in 1995.

largely prefer to follow my own instincts when it comes to dissecting the validity of criticism.

For many years a number of journalists on both sides of the Atlantic have reserved their most stinging vitriol for products of the German motor industry. Much of their ranting, although not all, could never be justified and a simple example will suffice here. In the summer of 1989 I was invited, along with hundreds of other journalists, by a leading German manufacturer, to the launch of a new car. Our aim was to test this car over several hundred miles in the Eifel Mountains and, as is normal practice on such occasions, we were sent off in pairs.

Through the winding hills and sharp hairpins my British 'partner' was clearly having dire problems. The right-hand rear wheel kept riding up over the high kerb stones through the corners, which was dangerous as this is the quickest way I know to invert a car onto its roof.

The reason was that the man at the wheel, who was reporting for a respected journal, had never previously driven a car with left-hand drive. It is a well-known characteristic of such folk that they have a tendency to turn into a corner too soon but, as far as this journalist was concerned, the car's steering was clearly to blame. I listened to him with increasing incredulity as he dealt the car one blow after another.

Clearly, he should not have been driving this car, let alone conveying his thoroughly inaccurate views about it in a national motoring magazine. But this was hardly an isolated incident. I have spoken to journalists, whose driving skills and writing ability I greatly admire, who have related similar stories, which is why I reiterate, I prefer to make my own judgement when appraising the integrity of a motor car, particularly when they are as beautifully thought out as a BMW.

1 Bayerische Motoren Werke: Flying High

FROM WINGS TO WHEELS

BMW's earliest days were spent producing aeroplane engines in Munich. Later the company ventured into engines for motorcycles, and by 1923 had launched its own motorcycle fitted with the classic and evergreen flat-twin. In 1928 it bought the Eisenach-based Dixi company, founded in 1896 to build Wartburg and Dixi motor cars. It was in 1928 that the first car constructed by BMW was launched but, as is well known, this wasn't a BMW at all – it wasn't even German – but an English Austin 7 made under licence.

This car was no more exciting than its British counterpart – the twin-cam supercharged Austin racers apart – but it did bring the delights of four-wheeled motoring to those who couldn't stretch to a Mercedes-Benz, Horch, Wanderer, DKW or Audi. The Austin 7 was also built in the United States (the Bantam), and in France (the Rosengart); it will come as little surprise to many that Datsun of Japan made an illegal copy of it.

By 1929 BMW had made several detail modifications to the Dixi, as it was dubbed in Germany and, right from the start of the year, attached the famous blue and white propeller badge to the top of the radiator surround. This wasn't an especially happy time for the German manufacturing industry, or anywhere else in the civilized world for that matter. The Great Depression of the early 1930s, largely caused by the financial crash on Wall Street, was just around the corner, and BMW's aero engine division began to suffer particularly badly.

Herbert Austin's 7 was a necessarily simple, even crude, motor car that provided little more than motorcycle facilities with two additional wheels. By the spring of 1932 BMW had finally ditched it in favour of the first all-BMW-built 3/20. This had a larger body than the Dixi, a chassis with a backbone chassis similar to that of the VW Beetle that Professor Porsche was developing in Stuttgart, and the engine had overhead valves and roller main bearings. Unlike the Beetle, that had swinging half-axles at the rear only, the BMW had this arrangement at the front as well and, in this respect, was well in keeping with contemporary German thinking.

In June 1933 the first 6-cylinder car, the 303, appeared. This was the first BMW to have the kidney-shaped radiator grille – still a hallmark of a BMW today – and also boasted a body made from pressed steel panels. The rear suspension, however, reverted to cart springs and a live rear axle instead of the previous model's swing axles.

Developing a paltry 30bhp this model was superseded in the spring of 1934 by the 4-cylinder 900cc 309 and 1.5-litre 6-cylinder 315. These were good solid machines with saloon bodies, a top speed in the region of 60mph and reasonable roadholding capabilities by the standards of the day. They

The famous blue and white 'propeller' badge denotes the company's roots in the aircraft industry, and has adorned every BMW car since 1928.

weren't particularly exciting cars, but had allowed BMW to weather the effects of the Wall Street disaster and establish a reputation for dependable engineering.

In Britain Bentley had stepped into financial oblivion and been absorbed by Rolls-Royce. Bugatti's dominance on European racing circuits had been toppled by Alfa-Romeo, who in turn were about to be comprehensively overthrown by the formidable onslaught of Daimler-Benz and Auto-Union. These Silver Arrows Grand Prix machines were truly revolutionary and caused a genuine sensation in the motor industry.

But in Germany at that time another engineering revolution was taking place, that would change the world as much as this country's cars. In 1932 one of the world's first motorways opened between Bonn and Cologne. Many more would follow, and car manufacturers rose admirably to the challenge of creating machines that would travel on them safely at high speed for long periods.

Above anything else it was the autobahn that, by the 1960s, had led the Germans to gain their unrivalled reputation for producing cars capable of astonishing mileages without wearing out or breaking. The autobahn network was undoubtedly responsible for the fast development of German motor cars. Many respected historians like Doug Nye argue, with conviction, that the banked racing track at Brooklands was responsible for stunting the development of British cars, particularly in the chassis and suspension departments.

The long-time editor of *Motor Sport*, Bill Boddy, a vociferous fan of Brooklands, refutes this claim wholeheartedly but he, unlike this author, did not have to endure a large chunk of his youth suffering bouts of travel sickness in the rear seat of a wallowing Alvis TA14.

A NEW SPORTS CAR

In 1934 BMW manufactured its first sports car, the 315/1 Sport, a triple-carburettor version of the 1500cc in-line six. The 319/1 Sport followed with a 1.9-litre triple-carburettor engine capable of propelling this little car up to an impressive top speed of nearly 80mph. Prolonged running at such speeds in a comparable British car invariably resulted in a snapped crankshaft and a set of 'dissolved' main bearings.

The 326 model followed in 1936 but by this time the BMW name had come to the attention of the Aldington brothers in Britain, who were Frazer Nash dealers. The

BMW's performance in the 1934 Alpine Rally impressed the British Aldington family to the extent that they imported these fine cars and marketed them here under the Frazer Nash BMW banner.

Frazer Nash was a crude, but fast and effective chain-driven British sports car. They still scare the living daylights out of Bentley drivers at historic race meetings today, but in the 1930s they made for relatively inexpensive rally and 'clubbie' race cars.

A team of these was entered for the 1934 Alpine Rally, where Alex von Falkenhausen, BMW's chassis engineer, competed in a BMW works-prepared 315/1. The Aldingtons were so impressed with his performance that they became importers of BMW cars and marketed them under the Frazer Nash BMW banner.

In the 326 Cabriolet and saloons sat a revised version of the in-line six; with a capacity of 1971cc it endowed the car with 70mph performance. It didn't matter that its acceleration was rather pedestrian – the car could travel at more than a mile a minute between German cities without groaning or boiling its radiator. When this same engine was fitted into the 328 two-

seater, debuted at the Nürburgring in prototype form during 1936, BMW had on its hands one of the world's truly great cars.

The 328 was a winner first time out – Henne averaging 67mph (101 kmh) over the course of the 70-mile race – and an enduring classic. Its light weight, advanced road manners, smooth engine and graceful beauty, put the 328 leagues ahead of virtually anything produced in its class at the time. English car collector and historian, Michael Barker, has campaigned his 328 in modern historic events for many years and, as a competent all-round sports car, rates it above everything else, including several Ferraris he's owned.

With 80bhp at a maximum of 4,500rpm the 328 was capable of nigh on 100mph, but it wasn't cheap to buy and just 462 examples were made before Hitler's antics in 1939 halted production. In various guises it scored many important victories in competition, including class wins in the Mille

Miglia, Le Mans and a famous outright victory by a streamlined version driven by Huschke von Hanstein and Walter Baumer in the 1940 Mille Miglia.

In the pre-War era it is the 328 for which BMW is most famously remembered. Its 6-cylinder engine was, of course, copied by Bristol and used for many years in the English car maker's roadgoing vehicles. Bristols were also great cars!

BMW were able to continue producing cars right up until 1941, but inevitably became embroiled in Adolf Hitler's war effort, producing arms, aero engines and the rest for the duration of hostilities. The 332 model was under way by the time Nazi storm troopers had become engaged in the unpleasant habit of kicking seven bells out of anyone their Führer took a disliking to, but, to all intents and purposes, it was stillborn.

GERMANY DEFEATED

In the aftermath of the War, when Germany was divided into a number of occupation zones controlled by the Allies, the lot of factory workers – mostly made up of German PoWs – was not especially happy. The established and great engineering names of pre-War Germany, including BMW and the Porsche concern (which wasn't able to make a sports car of its own until 1948), were ignominiously reduced to manufacturing household goods, utensils, garden tools and agricultural machinery.

Manufacturing motor cars was temporarily banned, except in Wolfsburg where Major Ivan Hirst of the Royal Electrical and Mechanical Engineers – an able and gifted Yorkshireman – was throwing his all into making the first 'proper' production Volkswagen Beetles.

BMW's factory at Milbertshofen fell into the American zone, where an order to demolish the building was luckily not carried out. Raw materials were in short supply, and the 1,000-strong workforce had to use whatever they could lay their hands on, and make something of what they could find. The company's governing custodian Dr Karl von Margoldt, a banker from Munich, was able to secure sufficient backing in the form of loans to allow the company to resume production, but cars would have to wait for the time being.

Motorcycles would have to come first, and towards the end of the decade business started to boom once again. Resurrection of the car division was a little more difficult, as the car factory at Eisenach was out of bounds, but the prospect of a fresh start held great advantages potentially.

A fine driver and gifted engineer, Alex von Falkenhausen was the driving force behind many of BMW's achievements both before and after the War.

LONG TIME WAITING

BMW's re-entry into the post-War car market didn't occur until 1951 when the big, heavy, bulbous 501 model was exhibited at the Frankfurt Motor Show. A 65bhp 4-door saloon, this car didn't go into production until 1952, and BMW would come to regret that it did, despite the launch of the more powerful 72bhp 501A version in 1954. The purchase price of the 510 – DM15,150 – was something of a stumbling block during a period in which an average office worker earned DM350 per month.

A 2.6-litre V8 was exhibited to the press and public at the 1954 Geneva Motor Show. The car was well received; it was noted for its smoothness, lack of mechanical noise and ability to reach 100mph. But it was not a success. In Germany it retailed at DM17,800 – the equivalent of £2,500 in Britain – at a time when an XK Jaguar sports car could be had for a little less than £1,700. Paradoxically, of course, William Lyons's Jaguar bore more than a passing resemblance to BMW's Mille Miglia-winning 328 streamlined car. And it was the Jaguar that captured the imagination of the British, Europeans and Americans alike.

BMW's efforts were something of a disaster, especially when compared to the fortunes of Daimler-Benz and Volkswagen. In Wolfsburg Volkswagen's profits proved that the company's chief executive, Heinz Nordhoff, had been correct in sticking with the inexpensive and relatively simple Beetle – the People's Car. Daimler-Benz provided nicely engineered, and reasonably priced saloons, but the situation of this great company was very different from BMW's.

After the War the people at Daimler-Benz were able to continue production at the long-established Sindelfingen factory just outside Stuttgart. By 1952 the financial situation of the company was so healthy that Daimler-Benz were able to enter their revolutionary 300SL 'Gullwing' sports cars for the Le Mans 24-Hours. Competitions manager Alfred Neubauer had led a factory delegation to Le Mans in 1951, where they saw a couple of English farmers, Peter Walker and Peter Whitehead, take victory at the Sarthe in a C-Type Jaguar. Mercedes returned the following year with the 300SLs and won. This car paved the way for the Austrian-born, American-based, sports car importer and dealer, Max Hoffmann, to put in an order for no fewer than 1,000 road-going versions of the 300SL (although there's no documentary proof of this), and the mighty Gullwing – a true 155mph motor car – sold well in spite of a very high price tag.

As post-War Germany began to recover economically, BMW's carmaking efforts stumbled, disturbingly, from bad to worse. Dubbed 'Baroque Angels', the big, fat V8 saloons continued in production. The 502 was launched in 1955 and, by 1958 had a 3.2-litre 120bhp version of the V8, and a top speed of 112mph. a 160bhp variant in the 3200S model pushed the top speed to 120mph.

To compete with the Mercedes-Benz 300SL Coupé of 1954 and 300SL Roadster version debuted in 1958, BMW slotted the V8 engine into their new 'supercar', the two-seater 507. A prototype of this car had appeared at the 1955 Frankfurt Motor Show, and most were agreed that it was a fine-looking machine. Available as a hard-top or Cabriolet, the Goertz-designed body was also exceptionally well made and engineered.

The V8's power of 160bhp at 5,000rpm gave the car a top speed ranging from 120mph to 138mph, depending upon which rear axle ratio was specified, but the car only added to BMW's problems. In every respect, this was an impressive sports car, but it was almost entirely handbuilt, and cost more to buy in America than the wickedly expensive Gullwing Mercedes-Benz. Predictably, production came to an abrupt halt after the 253rd example had rolled from the 'assembly' lines.

HANGING ON

At the 1955 Frankfurt Motor Show BMW also exhibited the first of the Isetta micro-cars. Powered by a 247cc motorcycle engine, this diminutive machine had a passable top speed of 55mph, for those who could stand the noise and vibration at such lofty velocity, and returned 42mpg. This was a timely introduction, as the Suez crisis hit hard in 1956. Almost all of Europe's car manufacturers – Volkswagen was a notable exception – felt its effects in some way or other due to fuel shortages.

The debut of the Isetta was also indicative of the ailing fortunes of BMW, particularly as the company's motorcycle-producing branch had also slipped into uncharacteristic decline. The Isetta was also powered by a 296cc engine; there was even a three-wheeler version built in Britain.

Microcars became big business, and even developed something of a 'cult' following, but profits for their makers were marginal. Once fuel rationing had ended in Europe, sales of these wondrous little machines also began to decline. A bigger 582cc 600 model was offered by BMW, and produced between 1957 and 1959. They sold reasonably well, and although small – they could just about seat four adults – it wasn't with a great deal of comfort.

This company 'fad' was followed in 1959 by the 700. This had smart bodywork by Michelotti, BMW's twin-cylinder motorcycle power unit but its production required a large bank loan, and the purchase of shares in the project by a timber merchant, Hermann Kruges. A conventional saloon with more interior space than the 600, the 700 was good for nearly 80mph.

The 1937 6-cylinder 319 sports model was so technically advanced that, apart from the inevitable vagaries of cross-ply tyres, it is still capable of showing a clean pair of heels to much more modern machinery.

Interestingly, it was faster than the Volkswagen Beetle, cheaper to run – 34mpg was easily obtainable – but, as was so often the case with BMW, the company just couldn't compete on price. Sales of the 700 saloon, and its pretty coupé sister, remained steady – 190,000 examples were made between 1959 and 1965, while those of the Beetle continued to spiral inexorably upwards. BMW's directors mused that the 700 was the model which would save the company from almost certain financial oblivion. But this was wishful thinking. It didn't. The only thing that could save the company was an injection of hard cash and little else.

FINANCIAL DIVERSION

The company's problems lay not just in declining motorcycle sales and miniscule profits from microcars. During 1955 the company started to build General Electric jet turbines. With a view to raising much-needed money it sold DM25 million worth of shares to MAN trucks. The venture was not successful and BMW lost money prior to pulling out.

In 1957 a new finance director, Heinrich Richter-Brohm, was installed to oversee BMW's fortunes. He and other members of the board had little cause to be optimistic about the company's future. It had simply not got the correct product to produce profits.

A typically neat innovation from the German manufacturer, the 315's toolkit is stored on the backrest of the driver's seat. Today's cars have their toolkits on the underside of the rear lid!

BMW had operated at both ends of the car-producing scale. On the one hand there were the expensive, powerful 'gas guzzlers' and on the other, 'oddball' microcars. A solution lay somewhere but BMW just didn't seem to be able to put their corporate finger on it. As affluence returned to Europe, the emergent middle classes that came with it, couldn't afford luxury cars and certainly didn't want motorized 'soap bubbles'.

Something in the middle, a quality but affordable saloon, was needed desperately if BMW was going to be saved from the fate that had befallen so many other German car manufacturers. Production of a mid-range car for the middle classes, however, could not be afforded. The Bavarian state government considered helping the company out with a DM10 million loan, but only on condition that Heinrich Richter-Brohm was removed from his position.

The banks involved also wanted the company's structure to change, so that shares could be taken up by both the banks and Daimler-Benz, and this was vigorously contested by BMW's shareholders. Richter-Brohm eventually resigned. The company was in a complete mess and troubled by 'internal wrangles', as companies are apt to be when in dire financial difficulties. And then a 'fairy godmother' stepped in in the form of Dr Herbert Quandt and his brother Harald, who bought a large shareholding in the company, installed Gerhard Wilke on the board, and began slowly to rebuild BMW's fortunes.

Under the influence of the Quandts, who would eventually secure control of the company, BMW rose from the depths of complete despair to the major force it is today. Recovery was fraught with difficulties at first, but gradually long-term investment made by the Quandt family was to pay exceedingly handsome dividends.

THE QUANDTS

The Quandt family established themselves in the Brandenburg town of Pritzwalk in the nineteenth century, having left Holland where they were famous as makers of rope. Emil Quandt bought a textile factory at the age of 34. His son Gunther was to follow in his father's footsteps, and eventually expanded the business to include wool, chemicals and arms production. Gunther had two children; they were Helmut (born 1908) and Herbert (born 1910).

In 1921 Gunther married a 19-year-old girl, Magda Friedlander, and they had a third son, Harald. Bored with her husband's business circumstances, Magda was soon fed up with him, and they divorced in 1929. She later married the Nazi party official, Josef Goebbels, and young Harald, who stayed with his mother, attended the wedding. Adolf Hitler was the best man! Inevitably, Harald was to spend a great deal of time at Goebbels's house near Berlin. He was just 10 years old when his mother married this Nazi monster, and became an innocent bystander in a hideous political regime.

At the outbreak of war in 1939 Harald was conscripted into the German army, and served as a lieutenant paratrooper. He saw active service in Crete and elsewhere, but was captured and spent a large chunk of the war in a Canadian PoW camp. Harald had six half brothers and sisters. They were Helga, Hilde, Helmut, Holde, Hedda and Heide.

When his mother and step-father discovered that Harald had been captured and was living in Canada, they wrote to him on several occasions. His mother's last letter, written from Hitler's bunker in Berlin when it had become obvious that Germany would lose the war, gave Harald an explanation as to why his mother, step-father, brothers and sisters would soon die. His mother wrote: 'They're too good for the life that will come after us and a merciful God will understand me when I give them salvation myself.' Josef Goebbels, of course, murdered the family and, later in life, Harald, quite understandably, would tolerate no mention of the evil man's name in his company.

After the war, which Gunther and Herbert also survived, this fabulously rich family went to work once again. In 1960 Herbert Quandt married his pretty secretary and personal assistant, Johanna Bruhn, who was 20 years his junior. Herbert had been married twice previously and had four children, but Johanna was utterly devoted to him. By this time Herbert and Harald had large business interests in the electrical, armaments and steel industries and a significant 14 per cent share in Daimler-Benz.

However, it was a meeting held in the Little Congress Hall in the Theresienhohe hills near Munich, on the cold evening of December 9 1959, that would not only add to the Quandt's fortunes, but also steer BMW away from bankruptcy. BMW's management team had recommended selling the company to Daimler-Benz, an idea that made BMW's shareholders audibly angry at the meeting.

Herbert Quandt stood on the sidelines and listened attentively and patiently to proposals and arguments put forward by those present. He was eventually asked by Kurt Golda of the works council if, as a potential investor in the company, there was anything he could do to avoid the impending probability of BMW's bankruptcy. Dogged by failing eyesight, but blessed with a sharp mind and acute hearing, Quandt hadn't thought very deeply at that time whether he could help or not, but considered that BMW's bankruptcy was the best option to be hoped for. Within three months, though, he had changed his mind, and quickly acquired 30 per cent of the company's shares at a reasonable price.

Having then spent some time restructuring the company, Quandt began to steer BMW in the direction that it had needed for quite some time. In later years Herbert's eyesight deteriorated further, as did his health, but his devoted wife Johanna supported him closely throughout. In the mid-1970s his eyesight all but disappeared, but this didn't prevent him and his wife taking dancing lessons, ostensibly in an attempt to restore his lack of balance. In 1982 he paid a visit to one of his children who lived in Kiel and died at Johanna's side.

The Quandt family were very private in their daily affairs; they had never sought publicity of any kind. It was Gunther who had coined the family motto: 'Never say anything. Avoid the public eye.' Its sentiments were close to Johanna's heart too. After her husband's death, she remained firmly in control of a company that was making huge profits. Almost overnight, she had become one of Europe's richest women. As such, she had also become an extremely influential and powerful figure, who controlled and made decisions about some of Germany's most successful economic concerns, including BMW.

Reputed to be worth more than £3 billion, it was Johanna's final decision that the company should acquire the Rover Group in January 1994, thus adding yet another of many strings to the Quandts' empirical bow. Shrewd but enigmatic, she lives a shy, retiring, almost reclusive life today. Like the vast majority of the world's elderly mothers, she values the company of her family above everything else, and only rarely appears in public.

Her annual appearance at Franfurt's Gravenbruch Castle Hotel to present a large

Pre-war saloons and cabriolets had a reputation for engineering quality, a relatively high purchase price and top-class performance, but 'tin-worm' has taken its toll and there are relatively few survivors.

cash prize to the journalist who, during the previous twelve months, has done most to promote public understanding of the private entrepreneur, is an occasion which she doesn't like to miss.

Although Johanna Quandt can ocasionally be seen doing her own shopping – she drives a 5-Series BMW – she is occasionally chauffeur driven in either a BMW or Mercedes-Benz. One or two top-ranking officals at Daimler-Benz once admitted that BMW make better engines.

Interestingly, when Herbert Quandt made his decision in 1960 to invest heavily in BMW, it was his, and not brother Harald's money that was used to buy the shares. This was, of course, something of a risk, but one that Herbert was prepared to take, because profits were huge. By 1967 the Quandt family found itself in a spot of bother as a result of an aeroplane crash in

the Italian alps in which Harald, aged 45, lost his life. There was financial danger lurking around the corner, as there often is in such circumstances.

The problem was that the family's power would have dwindled and declined sharply if their fortune had been divided up to cater for Harald's wife Inge and her five daughters. Harald's family finally received what was rightly theirs in 1974 when the family's share in Daimler-Benz was sold for £400 million.

Since his death in 1982 Herbert Quandt's widow and children have continued in the family tradition of creating wealth, with significant interests in a variety of companies on both sides of the Atlantic. During this same period, BMW sales have risen by more than 50 per cent, and the reasons for this are of the simplest nature – the company has wares that people want to buy!

TURNING POINT

It is widely acknowledged that there has never been anything seriously wrong with BMW's management team, designers or engineers. They have always been perfectly competent people, who possessed the characteristic German work ethic and natural desire for improvement. During the 1950s, they were merely victims of circumstance in search of the correct product. Success would eventually come as a result of financial investment, but there were teething troubles, not least of which was a dealer network resembling an 'over-patched' inner tube.

The 1961 Frankfurt International Motor Show marked something of a turning point in the company's history. It was here that BMW presented a new model – the 1500 saloon. This car had been hastily 'cobbled' together on a tight budget by people who, rather than spending their time in research and development, were given a simple brief to 'get on with it'. This was make or break time for BMW.

As an aside, it is coincidental that, in the world of Grand Prix racing, 1961 was the same year in which Sir Alfred Owen, head of the massive Owen organization in Britain, issued an ultimatum to BRM. If BRM failed to win a Grand Prix during 1962, Owen threatened to pull the financial plug on the whole racing team. Graham Hill duly won the Championship convincingly in 1962, and secured the team's future. Much the same sort of thing happened in Munich, although it was something of a slog to start with.

Of the new 1500 displayed at Franfurt one German magazine commented: 'Deep down, but nonetheless, there is a longing in the heart of the German car buyer for high quality, which can only be fulfilled by value-for-money, mass-produced cars.' This sentiment summarized exactly how BMW was perceived in Germany – a one-time manufacturer of bespoke carriages but, by the early 1960s, one that had been reduced to making a living in the new world.

For many the pre-War 328 was the finest 2-litre sports car ever made, its body styling providing William Lyons with inspiration for the Jaguar XK120. Capable of nigh on 120mph these cars continue to enjoy active service and success in classic car events today.

DISGRUNTLED CUSTOMERS

The assembly lines for the 1500 saloon started to churn over on August 25 1962, but the car was nowhere near ready for serious production. BMW's marketing man, Paul Hahnemann, who had joined the company from Auto-Union, knew this to be the case. He prepared himself, therefore, for adverse publicity – a barrage of telephone calls, telefaxes and letters from disgruntled customers.

Development of a new model usually takes approximately four years; the 1500 had taken less than two! Everyone involved in the project had pulled out all the stops to ensure that the 1500 happened but, as Hahnemann himself commented, the circumstances under which they all found themselves could only lead to what he described as a 'shit car'.

There was another problem as well. A German law made it compulsory for a car presented at a German motor show, which was intended for production, to go into production within six months of its public debut. Failure to comply was to invite potentially heavy financial penalties. On the day that a technician from the VDA (Association of the German Car Industry) arrived to give type approval to the new car, all hell broke loose at the factory.

Several 700 saloons were cleared from the assembly lines and around 20 handmade 1500 saloons were installed in their place. Technicians were transferred from one section to another in an attempt to fool the VDA tester into thinking, that they were working hard on production of the new car. This little trick just about worked but it was a close shave.

When production did finally happen it was hardly surprising that the car was riddled with faults. People working in the quality control department rejected one vehicle after another. And there was yet another hurdle, and one with which BMW was familiar. The company had originally envisaged a showroom retail price for the 1500 of DM8,500. As it turned out the cost could not be less than DM9,500, more than DM2,500 above that being asked for mid-range Fords and Opels. Customers, of course, were prepared to pay extra for a good quality vehicle, but the 1500 was hardly that. In particular, gearboxes and back axles broke one after another, and customers were far from amused.

The company did, however, have one piece of good luck. German manufacturers of good quality, quick, mid-range saloons, Borgward, went to the wall. BMW stepped immediately into its place and filled an important and potentially lucrative gap left by Borgward. This was convenient for BMW didn't want to compete with Ford and Opel, and couldn't at this stage have a go at Daimler-Benz who reigned supreme in the German luxury saloon market, but the Rover-cum-Alfa niche was growing year by year.

Alex von Falkenhausen, who had played an instrumental role in BMW's activities down the years, argued strongly in favour of propelling the new saloon with a 1.5-litre engine – the company wanted a 1.3-litre – and designed the power unit in such a way that it could easily be enlarged at a later stage to 1.8 and 2 litres.

A CHANGE IN RANGE

In 1962 production of the little Isetta 'bubble' car was finally halted, and the last of the 'Baroque Angels' followed a year later, finally putting paid to a part of the company's history that many would prefer not to remember. Quality problems were eventually and inevitably ironed out and, by

BMW's famous 2-litre in-line 6 that powered the 328 was also used as the basis for the engines that propelled post-War Bristols.

autumn 1963, BMW felt confident enough to launch the 1800 saloon.

This had an increase in engine power over the 1500, and also had its power unit canted over at an angle of 30 degrees. A sporting TI (Turismo Internationale) version was shown at the same time and, apart from an increase in performance, it was equally significant that the 1800 had a luxuriously appointed cabin – a portent of things ahead.

The attractive 700 saloon, coupé and rare cabriolet model was finally dropped from the range in 1965 after the production of 181,411 units. The following year the 2000 saloon arrived with revised rectangular headlamps instead of traditional circular ones, and there was a choice of a single carburettor 100bhp engine or 120bhp TI version. In Britain there was a Frazer Nash badged example but this didn't last long.

Also, in 1966 BMW launched the first of the beautiful CS Coupés. This was a 2-litre machine with bodywork by the Osnabrück-based coachbuilder, Karmann. The car had twin headlamps, a strong styling feature, that would remain on most, although not all, models right up to the present day. The CS was distinguished from its less exotically styled sisters by being made available with just two doors, while the ordinary saloon range had been offered in both two- and four-door guises right from 1962.

In recent times it has become almost fashionable to condemn the frontal appearance of the early CS. There is little justification for this but, of course, beauty in styling is very personal. By comparison with contemporary cars from Britain like the Ford Zephyr/Zodiac and Pininfarina-styled Morris Oxford and Austin Cambridge – all abominations in this author's view – the BMW was positively bristling with beauty.

By the mid-1960s things were looking up for BMW. The range comprised 11 models, namely, the 1600, 1800, 2000 and 2000CS, which were available in manual and automatic transmission forms and varying states of tune. Prices in the United States, where Max Hoffmann was selling every one he could lay his hands on, ranged from $2,613 for the 2-door 1600 to $5,265 for the 135bhp version of the 2000CS Coupé.

Then, as now, BMW and several journalists were keen to point out that the vast difference in purchase price between the 'entry level' model, and the range 'topper' was not on a sliding scale of engineering quality. All models were manufactured to the same high standards. By 1966 that standard was very high indeed, and BMW quickly regained its reputation – originally established in the 1930s – for producing sporting carriages of excellence. This wasn't before time, either.

In May 1967 *Road & Track* expressed a view that was wildly at variance with those of the owners of the early 1500s and commented:

> We've said it before but this seems an appropriate place to repeat it – Detroit simply isn't in the same league when it comes to combining ride and handling in the same suspension package. At the risk of becoming tiresome, let us say just once more that the BMW 1600 is a great automobile at the price. It retains all the good things that have made BMW one of our favourite cars and does it at a price that puts any number of other manufacturers to shame.

Herbert Quandt's idea – insistence – that providing real value for money was the only way in which BMW could successfully operate was beginning to pay off.

From 1967 the Baur-bodied 1600 Cabriolet was added to the range. This was a handsome if expensive piece, which found just 4,000 customers before production came to an end in 1975 to pave the way for the 3-Series. In 1968, however, the company pulled off a couple of masterstrokes in launching a brace of timeless classics that would not only rock Daimler-Benz's boat, but establish BMW owners as unofficial members of a global car club. These cars came in the form of the 2002 and 2800CS Coupé.

The 2002 was dubbed as such so as to avoid confusing it with the comparatively stolid 2000 saloon that soldiered on until 1972 before it was finally dropped from the range. The 2002 was basically the 1600–2 fitted with the 2-litre engine and, in such a lightweight body, went like stink. In essence there was little to touch it in its class, and BMW sales escalated both at home and abroad, particularly in North America, as a result. In the United States powerful engines in mid-range saloons were very much appreciated, as power-sapping exhaust emissions equipment became a legal requirement, and threatened the whims of enthusiastic drivers.

The big 2800CS Coupé was based on the earlier 2000CS Coupé, but fitted with the 2,788cc in-line 6-cylinder engine. Frontal styling was revised for the better and quietened critics of the 2-litre Coupé. This car was unashamedly aimed at the luxury sports market, and more particularly at the big Mercs. In America this car retailed at a whopping, but competitive, $9,000. By 1971 the engine capacity had grown to 2,985cc (the 3.0CS), which gave 180bhp on carburettors or 200bhp with

Bosch fuel-injected cars. Both manual and automatic transmission versions were capable of climbing into 130mph territory.

A lightweight version – a homologation special – with alloy body panels was launched in 1972 to allow BMW to take part in the European Touring Car Championship. Production was limited to just 1,039 cars with 39 examples of the special and outrageous 'Batmobile' versions being constructed between 1973 and 1975. With its huge rear wing and deep chin spoiler this quite amazing piece of equipment was a race car for the road, or vice versa, depending upon your point view.

Alongside the Coupés, there were the superb large saloons, the 2500, 2800 and 3.0 models, all of which played a major role in BMW's new-found fortunes. The 5-Series was launched in 1972 and the shortlived but formidable 2002 turbo appeared in 1973. But this classic era is not where our story ends. The Munich company continues to ride high, going from strength to strength. Success in motoring competition has hardly stopped since the days of the 328 before the War.

The current range of cars, from the 3-series to the mighty 850CSi, all arguably fall within most definitions of 'classic'. This is despite the incorrect and oft-quoted assumption that they are too new to be considered as such. A 'classic' car is a classic car, whether it was made a hundred years ago or yesterday. Cars do not automatically become classics, as many seem to think, after a certain and unspecified lapse of time.

In 1976 when the 1602 was replaced by the 3-Series, the older model was still highly regarded, and able to compete with newer

Crystal-clear instrumentation and an uncluttered dashboard were pre-War themes that have continued in the modern era.

designs from other manufacturers. There were some aspects of the design that naturally showed their age, but *Autocar*'s April 1975 road test summed up the car and BMW almost perfectly. The writer commented:

> The name of BMW has become well established in Britain in the last few years, enough to mean that some people will always want a car from Munich despite possible drawbacks. The 1602L certainly has some drawbacks, but not as many as its age might suggest. Its heating, ventilation and lighting could all be improved, while its performance, good by 1966 standards, is little better than average today. But its handling, its ride, its quietness and its finish still mark it out as a lot better than average; the question every buyer must ask himself is whether the high price is more than balanced by those factors.

From the pile of 'shit' launched in 1962, to the ultimate driving machine, the BMW story is an intriguing one indeed.

2 Rebirth of a Great Company

THE NEW AGE

The re-entry of BMW into the expensive, mid-range saloon car market was a brave gamble but one that had to be taken. Those with sufficiently long memories would inevitably compare the new sporting saloon with BMW's pre-War cars, and if the new didn't shape up to the old, the company would fade away. Those involved in the project knew this only too well.

Apart from this, there was no shortage of competition from British and other European car producers. For the time being the all-important North American market would have to wait; the new BMW had to be right in design if not in execution.

Foundations for the new car were actually dug out as early as 1958, and a 1600cc car was up and ready for testing and analysis by 1959. It turned out to be a complete 'pup'. The car was too heavy, too expensive, looked old-fashioned – the last thing BMW needed after the 'Baroque Angels' – and underpowered. This project was inevitably scrapped, Quandt money injected and the engineers and designers cleared out the thick cobwebs that lay in every corner of the company's back yard. The only similarities between the replacement design and that first prototype was that it had two doors, and a 4-cylinder engine driving the rear wheels.

What turned into the definitive BMW saloon had a 1500cc engine, a lighter and more aerodynamically efficient bodyshell, larger doors for easier access to the cabin, and a wholly fresh and modern feel. It had shed significant quantities of weight, was so obviously European in origin – an important selling point in the United States – and arguably most interesting of all, had a large window glass area.

The reason behind the latter was obviously to improve safety, but unbeknown to BMW's people, Rudi Uhlenhaut and Bela Bareyni – Daimler-Benz's top development specialists – were concurrently developing a special vehicle over in Stuttgart scheduled for launch in 1963. This was the 230SL sports car, a revolutionary piece of engineering that broke new ground in performance, handling and safety.

It was unusual in that its window glass area was also extremely generous, again for reasons of safety. With a normal flat roof panel the car would have looked somewhat gawky, a problem that was solved easily by creating a roof pressing, that was lower in the centre than the necessarily high sections on the outsides. It is doubtful that BMW's engineers knew anything about the important work by Uhlenhaut and Bareyni in the field of primary safety. It is more likely that the 1500 simply evolved into the modern age of the 1960s, but it's an intriguing coincidence nevertheless.

Changes between prototype stage and production were minimal, but included an increase in the diameter of the road wheels from 13in to 14in, and increase in engine oil

Like the modern 3 and 5 series, the great BMWs produced before Hitler's lunacy were superb all-round sports cars, equally at home on road and track.

capacity of just 2 pints. In all other respects the design was considered to be about right, and this was borne out by the model's relatively long production run of ten years.

It had long been a part of German automotive thinking that 'niche marketing' was a key strategy. To this end there was a deliberate policy at BMW of sticking to a design, and making production modifications as and when they became necessary. Launching new models at regular intervals, as the Japanese, for example, do today was anathema throughout the whole German motor industry. It was a policy that was particularly appreciated by customers who bought German cars for their distinctive national character. The BMW 1500 was positively brimming with German character.

THE 'FULL-BODIED BIMMER'

Available in two- and four-door guises the all-steel unitary construction hull was to a conservative, three-box design with styling undertones from the Michelotti-penned BMW 700 model. With its distinctive 'overhanging' bootlid, deep swage lines along the sides of the body and doors, and boldly shaped rear side windows, BMW had captured a style that would make future models instantly recognizable.

In profile, the car appeared to 'slope' forwards, the front and rear being steeply raked. This gave an aggressive, almost shark-like appearance that would become a distinctive feature of future BMWs. Front to rear weight distribution worked out at 53.5/46.5, a commendable achievement, which endowed the car with pleasant, safe and predictable handling characteristics. Heavy wrap-around bumpers fitted with overriders front and rear were in the vogue of the day but, as the later racing cars revealed, these cars looked more aesthetically correct without them.

The bodyshell was entirely conventional in construction, and made from a series of panels welded, rather than bolted, together. Separate pieces were used for the sills, or rockers, inner wings, roof and floor pans. The rear outer wings were welded to the body, while the front ones were bolted – a tradition that continues today.

BMW 1500 (1962–64)

Chassis   Unitary construction

Engine
Type   In-line
Block material   Cast-iron
Head material   Alloy
Cylinders   Four
Cooling   Water
Bore × stroke   82 × 71mm
Capacity   1,499cc
Valves   Two
Timing   Single ohc
Compression ratio   8.8:1
Maximum power   80bhp at 5,700rpm
Maximum torque   87lb ft at 3,200rpm
Fuel system   Single Solex 34 PICB carburettor
Fuel tank capacity   14gal (64ltr)

Transmission
Gearbox   Four-speed synchromesh with drive through a conventional propshaft to the rear wheels
Ratios   First 3.82
                                 Second 2.17
                                 Third 1.36
                                 Fourth 1.00
                                 Reverse 4.15
                                 Final drive 4.38
Clutch   Fichtel & Sachs single dry-plate

Suspension and Steering
Front   Independent by MacPherson struts, coil springs and anti-roll bar
Rear   Independent by triangular trailing arms and coil springs
Steering   ZF Gemmer worm and roller with 3.3 turns from lock to lock
Tyres   6.00x14 crossply
Wheels   Vented pressed steel
Rim width   14in

Brakes   Hydraulically operated Dunlop discs (front), drums (rear)

Dimensions (in/mm)
Track   Front 52/1,320
                                 Rear 54/1,366
Wheelbase   100/2,550
Overall length   177/4,500
Overall width   67/1,710
Overall height   57/1,450
Dry weight   2,337lb (1,060kg)

Performance
Maximum speed   96mph (154km/h)
0–60mph (0–100km/h)   14sec
Standing quarter mile (0.4km)   19sec
Fuel consumption   25–32mpg (8.8–11.3ltr × 100km)

For variations relating to the later 1600, 1800 and 2-litre models, refer to the main text

The amount of bright trim used externally would be considered distasteful and excessive by today's standards, but was entirely in keeping with contemporary trends. Bright mouldings were attached around the perimeter of the windows and trailing edge of the rear lid. Chromium plating was applied to the hubcaps (embossed with BMW badges at their centres), the radiator grille, circular headlamp bezels, and a further moulding around and between the interestingly styled stop and tail-lamps.

Unlike the majority of its contemporaries the bonnet was front-hinged and, although this slightly restricted access to components like the water radiator, it was another important safety consideration. The large rear lid, the lock for which was located on the transverse rear panel, gave access to a truly enormous boot. Its roughly rectangular shape lent itself particularly well to swallowing the biggest suitcases and squashy bags, but some journalists criticized the location of the spare wheel in a purpose-formed horizontal well in the boot floor close to the fuel tank. This, claimed some commentators, was a backwards step, as a boot full of luggage would cause extreme inconvenience in the event of a puncture.

With the wisdom of hindsight the critics, although they had a point, were wrong. As modern market research shows, the vast majority of motorists rarely fill their boots with anything bulkier than four carrier bags of supermarket produce, and it was much the same situation in 1962.

In launching the 1500, BMW weren't so much giving notice of the success the company so badly needed, as hinting at their quiet confidence for the future. The kidney-shaped radiator grille was in place, as were the distinctive circular headlamps and BMW badges front and rear, but there was no room for complacency at this stage.

Cabin Cruiser

Roomy, comfortable and generously appointed, the interior made good use of space and, in some respects, was well ahead of its time. There were, for example, seatbelt anchorage points that were by no means standard on all cars at this time. The vinyl-covered seats were also deeply padded, and more reminiscent of a 1950s Bentley than of a car attempting to extricate its makers from financial difficulties.

The front seats were adjustable fore and aft, and gave reasonable support in most directions, although for 'door handle' cornering, a little more lateral support would have been useful. This point led *Car & Driver*'s testers to remark: 'We hope that BMW will see their way to making Reutter seats (or similar) optional equipment.'

Dubbed the 'Baroque Angels', BMWs of the immediate post-War period were large, powerful, thirsty, expensive and destined to failure. The fortunate few with money to spend usually plumped for a Mercedes-Benz, Alvis or Bentley.

et
al
to
at
ld
m

ty
le
sts
at
by
va-
ng
ad-

was also part of a trend that continues in the German motor industry today, that they were kept as simple as possible, so as not to distract the driver from exercising his craft.

This simplicity in layout was in contrast to contemporary British and Italian cars that were noted for multiple instrumentation, and sundry planks of glossy wood placed at strategic intervals around the interior.

The two-spoke steering wheel was a typically large – too large – item with finger grips on the underside of the rim and a chromed semi-circular horn ring in the lower segment. This was hardly a sporting feature of the car, but potential converts from Mercedes-Benz had come to expect a wheel of truck-like dimensions, and BMW were only too happy to oblige them.

The pedal arms were unusually long and top-hinged, but slightly offset towards the centre of the car. It was an arrangement that took a little getting used to, except for

Rear styling of the 1950s 501/502 series was bulbous, ungainly and a far cry from the simple elegance of the pre-War cars.

owners of right-hand drive Volkswagens, who had long since taken to this odd arrangment.

With its vinyl-covered top surface and plain, painted metal finish, little imagination had gone into the style of the dashboard and, considering the sporting nature of the car, a tachometer was conspicuously absent. However, all the 'essentials' were in the right place and within easy reach.

The instrument binnacle comprised a circular speedometer with integral distance recorder to the left of the steering column, a small clock in the centre, and a combination instrument on the right. The latter included a fuel gauge, oil pressure warning light, water temperature gauge and dynamo warning light.

Car & Driver's testers commented:

> It would be wrong for BMW to use anything but proper dials for the instrument panel, so we were glad to find large and legible round instruments. But in addition to the almost necessary tachometer, we missed an oil pressure gauge (there's just a warning light). The dash pad comes forward to provide some hooding for the instruments so that there are never any reflections from them in the windshield. The panel light has a rheostat switch for brightness.

Such a switch is fitted to virtually all modern cars today, but this was something of a novelty in all but the most expensive luxury saloons in the early 1960s.

In the centre of the dashboard were horizontally positioned slides for controlling heating and ventilation, with the windscreen wiper knob and cigar lighter to their left and right, and a glovebox on the extreme right. The headlamp flasher unit and indicators were operated by stalks protruding from the left and right of the steering column, and the main headlamp switch was conveniently positoned on the left of the dashboard. In addition to these functions, there was a manual choke button on the console, and a combined ignition/starter switch integrated into the right-hand side of the steering column.

Bright mouldings ran almost the entire width of the dashboard, adding a touch of luxury, and a flexible grab handle was fitted above the glovebox for the benefit and safety of nervous passengers. It's difficult to appreciate the role of a grab handle in the event of a collision, but BMW obviously deemed one to be worthwhile. Unlike BMW's big bulbous saloons of the 1950s that had a column-mounted gearshift, the 1500's lever rose from the centre of the floor and had a knob that was conveniently close to hand.

As far as the interior was concerned the designers had performed an excellent job. The car was priced considerably above many others in the 1.5-litre mid-range category, but BMW's management were uncompromising in their belief, that there was an untapped market for luxury in a smaller package than Daimler-Benz or Alvis could provide.

Decreasing Circles

Where wheel and tyre technology are concerned, nearly all car makers except Daimler-Benz continued to dabble in the 'dark ages'. In Stuttgart Daimler-Benz's chief development engineer Rudi Uhlenhaut had engaged tyre makers, Continental, to produce a new radial tyre capable of coping with the potential cornering power of the chassis and suspension under the 230SL sports car.

In Britain the Herefordshire rally driver, Bill Bengry, was busy helping Pirelli to develop the Cinturato (née Cintura) radial-ply tyre, and Michelin had proved beyond doubt with their X tyre, that radials were

1950s opulence appealed to the sybaritic, but BMW just couldn't find sufficient customers to make their efforts worthwhile.

superior tyres to crossplies in every respect. Despite these exciting developments, BMW fitted 14×6.00 Metzeler crossplies, which was almost unforgivable for such a well-engineered costly vehicle.

Rather plain vented 4.5J steel wheels were employed and had a four-bolt attachment to the hubs. Alloy wheels would have been preferable, of course, but these weren't in general use at this time, and it's difficult to imagine such an 'upright' saloon looking kindly on the sort of spoked wheels beloved of so many British manufacturers. In deference to the humdrum appearance of the wheels, the chromium-plated hubcaps and vented alloy wheel trims brightened up the car's appearance considerably.

A 'Quad-Pot'

For a company that had produced such fine, small capacity 6-cylinder engines before the War, the choice of an in-line 4-cylinder was something of a gamble, but there were good reasons for this. There was no denying the inherently superior smoothness and balance of a 6-cylinder – nor the glorious exhaust note – but BMW's engineers wanted a shorter power unit, that could be placed as far forward in the chassis (above the cross-member) as possible.

This would create understeer during hard cornering, which was considered safer for drivers of average ability, and also make the car more stable at high speeds during crosswinds. In addition, it would make it more stable and predictable during hard braking, as loads were heavily concentrated on the front wheels.

A 4-cylinder engine was also cheaper to manufacture, took less time to assemble and service, and gave significantly improved fuel consumption. It was for all these reasons that the motor industry generally was moving away from small capacity 'sixes' and 'eights', although Triumph persisted with a small 6-cylinder in the Vitesse and GT6 sports models for several years.

The power unit in the BMW was canted over to the right-hand side at an angle of 30 degrees, which held the advantage of both lowering the bonnet line and centre of gravity. There was nothing new in this approach; Daimler-Benz had used the same arrangement in the 3-litre 6-cylinder-engined 300SL sports car during the 1950s and it worked extremely well. To some it just looked a little odd by comparison with conventional upright engines. But BMW knew perfectly well that the vast majority of customers would never have any inclination or reason to venture under the bonnet, let alone get involved in any intellectual engineering discussions over a glass of sherry as to the correct angle of a power unit.

The engine's architecture was one that BMW have largely adhered to in their passenger saloons to this day, and comprised an alloy cylinder head bolted to a cast-iron cylinder block and a narrow gauge steel sump pan. Light alloy was used for the inlet manifold, pistons, gearbox casing and clutch bellhousing to save weight.

The big Bee-ems of the 1950s had performance and looks to match the luxury Jaguars, but lost out badly to the Coventry concern on price. Munich's best cost almost double in the showroom!

The crankshaft sits in five main bearings and drives an overhead camshaft via a self-adjusting chain. It also drives the oil pump, whereas drive for the fuel pump and distributor is from the camshaft. A plastic cooling fan at the front of the engine is driven by a 'V' belt that also propels the dynamo and water pump. Thick-walled water jackets around the cylinders were used to minimize cylinder wear and withstand the expansion effects of heat building up.

To a conventional design, the camshaft operates rockers to open and close the eight valves; the latter were inclined at an angle of 55 degrees. Fuel was dispensed to the bores by a single Solex 34 PICB carburettor with a manually operated choke and, despite a relatively high compression ratio of 8.8:1, the engine was capable of running perfectly happily on 95 octane fuel.

With a bore and stroke of 82×71mm (3.23×2.80 cu in), the engine was 'over-square' in keeping with contemporary trends, and had an overall capacity of 1,499cc (91 cu in). Maximum power of 80bhp was developed at 5,700rpm and maximum torque of 87lb/ft at 3,200rpm. This endowed the car with a top speed of around 95mph, with the 0–60mph dash from rest taking a minimum of 14secs. By the standards of the day these figures were quite astonishing for a 1.5-litre-engined car. By comparison, the Volkswagen Beetle 1500 (1,493cc) launched in 1966 (Germany's best-selling saloon in 1967), developed 44bhp and had a top speed of around 78mph.

Of the BMW, *Car & Driver* commented:

The engine is quiet in operation, and its willingness to reach and sustain high rpm is perhaps its most endearing feature. It just never seems to stop accelerating, and will reach 7,000rpm in the gears with remarkable ease. Unfortunately, a tachometer is not standard equipment, and should at least be made an optional accessory . . . No vibration from engine or drivetrain penetrated to the driver or passengers at any time, and the soft engine mountings are perhaps mainly responsible for this. You may get an idea of how quiet the car really is from the fact that Julius Weitmann, staff photographer, fell asleep in the back seat on an Autobahn stretch on which we averaged 90mph.

Four on the Floor

Drive to the rear wheels was through a Fichtel & Sachs single dry-plate clutch, and 4-speed Porsche-type gearbox with synchromesh on all four forward speeds. Many journalists considered this to be the best 'box to be found anywhere. It was impossible to beat the synchromesh, and most of them praised the change for its lightness in use.

Gearbox ratios were as follows: First 3.82:1, Second 2.17:1, Third 1.36:1, Fourth 1:1, reverse 4.15:1 (no synchromesh), Final Drive 4.38:1.

Car & Driver's testers commented:

This is a very pleasant transmission, the only possible complaint being the exaggerated spacing between second and third gears, and the placing of the gear lever slightly too far forward. Drivers who hold the wheel with straight arms will have to take one shoulder off the backrest to reach first and third. On the credit side the gate is the most precise of any floor-shift car made in Germany.

The gearbox was intended to be in keeping with the car's sporting nature, but the high-ratio third gear – also a feature of the Porsche 356 and VW Beetle – placed heavy demands on the second ratio, which is one reason why so many early gearboxes and rear axles failed these otherwise splendid cars.

Strutting out

It was obvious to all who drove the 1500 from the off, that the chassis and suspension were capable of handling considerably more than anything the engine could hurl at them. All four wheels were independently and relatively firmly sprung, even by German standards.

At the front there were MacPherson struts – BMW was among the first car makers to utilize these – wishbones, coil springs and an anti-roll bar. At the rear the differential housing was bolted directly to the underside of the body, and the narrow driveshafts were articulated with universal joints on their inner ends.

Large triangular trailing arms were used for locating the wheels, with springing being taken care of by vertical coils mounted on top of the trailing arms. The shock absorbers were bolted to the bodywork, and to the trailing arms at the bottom and inclined forwards at a steep angle. This rear set-up was similar in design to the little 700 model's, with the wheels moving through 3.15in during compression and 4.54in on rebound. Maximum travel at the front was 3.36in in both compression and rebound.

The suspension system was both relatively simple and light, and in stark contrast to the heavy transverse torsion bars favoured by Porsche for the 356 model. In normal circumstances the BMW had neutral handling characteristics, tending towards understeer when approaching the limit of adhesion. Skilled drivers, however, soon learned that late braking and wide throttle openings turned understeer into delightful quantities of very controllable oversteer, particularly in second and third gears. It was this capability that earned BMW a reputation for building 'driver's' cars. The passage of time has done nothing to diminish this reputation.

In conjunction with ZF worm-and-roller steering the car was easy to throw around, despite the low gearing (3.5 turns of the wheel from lock to lock), and 32ft turning circle. The 1500's ability to stop was of a similarly high order, courtesy of 10.5in Dunlop discs at the front and 10in-diameter drums at the rear. Braking was about the only area of design in which the Germans trailed behind Britain during the 1950s. Dunlop were at the forefront of disc development, and it is to BMW's credit that they recognized this. Even without servo assistance the brake pedal required very little pressure, the brakes proved to be fade-free – not the case with the bulky Baroque Angels – and pulled the car up straight and true from maximum speed . . .

Good start . . . bad start

Despite having been cobbled together in such a short period of time, the overall design of the 1500 was sound, even if build quality was wanting in certain areas, but it marked the beginning of BMW's recovery in an increasingly competitive motoring world. In all, 23,807 people parted with large quantities of cash for the new 1500. They might otherwise have bought a Lancia or Alfa-Romeo, two of the relatively few companies producing high-performance sporting saloons with above average price tags.

The engineers in Munich lost little time in sorting out the 1500's teething troubles. They had to, because the future success of the company was dependent upon convincing potential customers that a BMW was a better bet than a Volvo 122S or Lotus Cortina, both of which offered excellent performance and good handling in a four-seater bodyshell.

All things considered, BMW had made a reasonably good start, and began to cultivate an image in its chosen niche market.

Launched at the 1955 Frankfurt Motor Show the Isetta 'bubble car' enabled BMW to ride the 1956 Suez crisis, but profits were miniscule. By 1959 the great company was heading in the direction of the bankruptcy courts.

The company's 'hand-out' advertising literature for the 1500 – a single piece of paper folded in the middle – revealed that:

The BMW 1500 was borne of tradition and progress. It unites decades of experience in automobile construction with the newest technical developments. All demands that you can make on a fast touring car today and tomorrow are fulfilled by the BMW 1500: safety, performance, riding comfort, beauty – and above all roadholding – outstanding and exemplary.

These were extravagant claims, although not especially exaggerated, but BMW didn't really believe the 1500 to be the be-all-and-end-all of everything, because the company announced a more powerful 1800 version at the 1963 Frankfurt Motor Show.

EXPANSION BEGINS

Externally, the larger-engined model was distinguished by a chromed strip across the side of the bodywork, and under the right foot by an increase in performance. In BMW's publicity literature it was distinguished by a higher price tag of DM9,985 – that is, DM500 more than the 1500 version.

The increase in engine capacity was achieved by the relatively simple expedient of increasing the bore and stroke to 84mm×80mm (3.31×3.15cu in) to give an

On the brink of financial oblivion in 1959, Dr Herbert Quandt (right) invested heavily in BMW and saved the company from an almost certain demise.

overall capacity of 1,773cc (108cu in). The compression ratio was lowered to 8.6:1, and a larger single Solex 36–40 PDSI carburettor was fitted. These 'tuning' measures conspired to give a maximum 90bhp at 5,250rpm, sufficient to propel the car to a maximum speed of 105mph. The small increase in power was offset by worthwhile gains in torque.

Power-assisted steering was a new feature, although not strictly necessary, and automatic transmission was offered as an extra-cost option. However, it was the TI version, announced at the Frankfurt Motor Show in 1963 and scheduled for series production from February 1964, that caused the biggest stir among BMW enthusiasts.

This model took the company's sporting aspirations several steps further and launched BMW into the 'mainstream' of sporting manufacturers. If the original 1500 had been something of a wolf in sheep's clothing, the 1800TI was something approaching a tiger in the same skin. Praise from journalists for this model was indeed generous, because this was one of the world's few saloons that had genuine performance akin to a 'proper' sports car. And, unlike its 'baby' sister, it didn't break gearboxes and rear axles.

Apart from an alternator and stronger connecting rods, the TI had the same engine as the 'cooking' 1800 model including a shared camshaft. But the superior power – 110bhp at 5,800rpm – was found by increasing the compression ratio to 9.5:1, and bolting on a brace of Solex 40 PHH horizontal carburettors. Both versions of the 1800 were also available with 165×14 radial tyres and a rear anti-roll bar that transformed the car's roadholding and handling capabilities.

The gear ratios were also altered as follows: First 3.82:1, Second 2.07:1, Third

1.33:1, Fourth 1:1, Reverse 4.15:1, Final-drive 4.11:1.

Most road test reports reckoned the TI to be good for between 107–110mph. Sprinting ability from rest to 60mph at maximum revs took a whisker or two above 11secs, which was excellent considering the overall weight of the vehicle. But this had to be paid for, naturally, as fuel consumption with a light right foot was little better than 23mpg, and could dip to as low as 16mpg if the car was exploited to the full. But this, all said and done, was what the car was for.

In some respects the 1800TI was in a class of its own. Like the Volvo 122S, the BMW was conservatively styled, but the latter was faster than a Porsche 356 1600 up through the gears, just losing out to the Stuttgart car on top speed. Some described the BMW as being as comfortable and effortless as a Citroën DS, as roomy as the Farina-designed Peugeot 404 and as agile as a Mini Cooper S.

It lacked the refinement and ride comfort of the elegant but relatively pedestrian Rover 2000, but cost almost as much to buy as a Porsche 356. This was not something that particularly mattered to BMW's board or their marketing people. A high purchase price was not considered to be a major drawback, because it was becoming increasingly obvious as the 1960s unfolded, that certain sections of European and American society were becoming much more affluent.

To endorse their faith in the potential of expensive sporting saloons, BMW launched a limited production run of just 200 specially equipped 1800TIs with a hefty purchase price of DM13,500 each. They were intended solely for racing, and almost all were sold to racing drivers.

Externally, these were no different from the regular TI but, under the skin, there was a 5-speed gearbox, limited-slip differential and a choice of four different rear axle ratios. Engine revisions included a high compression ratio of 10.5:1 and twin Weber H5 DCOE carburettors, which pushed maximum power output to 130bhp at 6,100rpm.

The success of these cars in European Touring Car racing did nothing but good for BMW's image, and sales of the 'ordinary' road cars began to increase markedly. Not that BMW were in the 'volume' market in the Ford and Opel sense of 'moving metal' as fast as possible. BMW's purpose was to go fast in a very different direction, and the Americans were particularly quick to catch on.

So impressed were *Car & Driver*'s staff with the 1500 in 1963, that they could hardly wait to get their hands on the 1800TI. They failed to find fault with it, except for the revised steering wheel which, with its full circular horn ring was described as 'not what you'd call handsome'. By April 1965 when this magazine's report was published, BMW had got around to fitting a tachometer to the TI version as standard equipment; in this respect, BMW had been a little more rapid to react to constant press criticism than some branches of the German motor industry.

The writer of the American journal's report considered the BMW to be an ideal machine for someone who, for a variety of reasons, couldn't choose between an out-and-out sports car or a luxury saloon. With the ability to cruise at speeds above 100mph, without excessive wind noise or 'crashing' on and off bumps and potholes in the tradition of classic British sports cars, for example, the BMW was, according to *Car & Driver*, nothing short of being a 'super saloon'.

The report's writer commented:

The quality control is amazing when you consider that it's put together by Bavarians, who are all individuals and not much given to the regimentation of mass-production lines. There is evidence of great care in craftsmanship, which probably involved more specialized hand labour than any sedan short of a Maserati Berlina ... Finally the BMW is economical and reliable. It shouldn't need much attention or service, but when it does, Hoffmann Motors (the US distributors) stand ready to render prompt assistance. This much maligned company has made great strides in the past few years and we have no reservations about recommending them as a sales and service organization.

As an aside this latter comment is interesting, because motor industry experts for years have expressed surprise, and even bewilderment, at the unrivalled success of the Volkswagen Beetle over three decades. Apart from the Beetle's virtues of reliability, durability and low purchase price and running costs, Volkswagen's chief executive up until his death in 1968, Heinz Nordhoff, insisted upon a large dealer network, that provided near perfect service and stocked large quantities of spare parts.

No-one ever became a Volkswagen dealer without being prepared to carry large stocks of components – a heavy financial burden for dealers – but it was a policy that worked well. It was a policy whose value BMW had failed to appreciate in the past, but they quickly made up for the shortfall by the mid-1960s.

1500 DROPPED

In March 1964 the 1500 was superseded by the 1600, the increase in engine capacity having been achieved by an increase in the cylinder bore diameter by 2mm to bring it up to 84mm. At 71mm the stroke was the same as the 1500's and the overall capacity worked out at 1,573cc. In conjunction with a single Solex 36–40 PDSI carburettor, this gave the 1600 a 3bhp gain in power over the 1500 and a slight increase in torque, but this model was not particularly successful.

Despite its inevitably higher purchase price, BMW enthusiasts voted with their pockets and plumped for the 1800. Between 1964 and 1966 the 1600 found 10,278 customers, whereas 102,090 1800s were made up to 1968. Surprisingly, the expensive 1800TI outsold the 1600 by almost two to one with 19,663 units being produced up to 1966.

As had been established when the 1500 engine was designed, this amazingly strong power unit was capable of being 'bored out' to a full 2 litres. The 2000 version debuted in 1966. With a bore and stroke of 89×80mm, this 1,990cc unit in standard form developed a respectable 100bhp at 5,500rpm, and breathed through a single Solex 40 PDSI carburettor.

Externally, the 2000 was distinguishable from the 1800 by its rectangular headlamps, a styling whim that many considered made the car look ugly. More accurately, it was distinctively mid-European, and did not adversely affect sales. In addition to the 'entry-level' car, the 2000 was also made in 5-speed TI and Tilux guises, and there were 3-speed automatic versions of each.

Both the TI and Tilux versions had twin Solex 40PHH carburettors and produced 120bhp at 5,500rpm. And whereas the standard 2000 had a compression ratio of 8.5:1, the two quicker models had their ratios raised to 9.3:1. The Tilux (or Ti Lux), which retailed in Germany at more than DM1,000 above the 'cooking' 2-litre car, was, as its name suggested, the luxury version and boasted a walnut veneer dashboard, plusher upholstery and twin headlamps. To cope

Captured here in 1969 Johanna Quandt remains at the helm of the Munich car giant in 1999, and is among the world's richest women.

with the extra power the quicker versions were also fitted with 175×14 radial tyres, whereas the ordinary version made do with 165×14s.

BUILDING NICE CARS

The use of wooden trim in the Tilux's interior was something of an oddity for a German car at this time. But, as *Road & Track*'s 1967 road test pointed out:

> This is done in a restrained, modern finish, not the overdone high gloss varnish favored by most manufacturers who use genuine wood trim. The same wood theme is carried out within the instrument centres though one of our nitpickers peered closely and triumphed, 'The grains don't quite match'

As in the past *Road & Track* staff found little to complain about. They criticized the pedals for being too small and close together, and called for a stronger spring on the gear lever to prevent accidental selection of reverse when trying to get bottom gear. One journalist managed to jam his thumb nail in the window winder. But these were small niggles and a small price to pay for a car which, in all other respects, was almost impossible to criticize.

To improve ride quality the Tilux had slightly softer suspension than the TI version, mainly for the benefit of the American market, and although bodyroll was more pronounced during hard cornering, the car was rarely given to losing composure.

Road & Track commented:

> The overall ride of the 2000 Tilux is perhaps its most endearing quality. On a typically smooth American highway, almost any car on the road delivers an acceptable ride. It is when the surface is less than perfect that such excellent suspensions as the BMW

come into their own and on really bad, patchy road surfaces, the BMW's ride is fantastic.

It is interesting that original, or well-restored examples today, bear up well by comparison with their modern counterparts, although there's no denying the huge strides forward in tyre technology during the 1990s. *Road & Track* concluded:

> BMW build nice cars. Always has. And the more of them we drive, the more we appreciate them. R&T publisher John R. Bond lists the BMW as one of his Seven Best cars and though the entire staff might not agree with his choice of all seven, none would disagree that BMW deserves its position in that distinguished company.

BMW's rise in fortunes in such a relatively short period was truly astonishing. By 1969 the company had celebrated production of its millionth car – a 2000. By Volkswagen Beetle production standards, which were nearly a million units annually by this time, BMW's output was miniscule, but very healthy considering the kind of market the company had carved out for itself. Jokes about 'bubble cars' had been all but forgotten, in the same way that jokes about Skodas were dropped when Volkswagen took over the Czechoslovakian concern.

GOING PLACES

These cars provided a strong hint of the direction in which BMW were heading. The company had learned a hard lesson during the 1950s. The production of large, heavy, expensive luxury saloons was not a good idea during economically challenging times.

When western economies began to boom, as they did towards the end of the 1960s, though, luxury cars for which people were prepared to pay large amounts of money came into their own. Not that the company was about to risk putting its eggs all in one basket.

The 2000 soldiered on until 1972, the TI and Tilux versions being discontinued in 1968 and 1972 respectively. They had served their purpose extremely well, but the body styling had begun to look a little dated by the mid to late 1960s. Modifications were made to keep them looking fresh; the 1800 had a partially black-painted radiator grille and brushed chrome hubcaps from 1968 and, in 1971, close to the end of production, the radiator grille was painted wholly in black. There was also a revised dashboard with hooded instruments, a larger 3-spoke steering wheel with a larger horn button at its centre, and the same rectangular head-lamps fitted to the 2000.

In 1969 the 2000 was fitted with Kugelfischer PL04 fuel injection and dubbed the Tii. Fuel injection was gradually beginning to replace carburettors across the industry at this time, as a means of producing more efficient combustion and cleaner exhaust emissions.

This was especially important in California, where smog caused largely by car exhausts was having an adverse effect on the population's health. This led to legislation that forced manufacturers to clean up their acts. The emissions equipment that accompanied most fuel-injection systems, however, normally sapped significant quantities of engine power and, as the 2000 Tii developed only 10bhp more than the twin-carburettor model, it was not a great success. A total of 1,922 cars was made before production was halted in 1972.

3 Making a Classic

A MASTERSTROKE

From the mid-1960s, the company diversified and extended the range of cars with the launch of two quite extraordinary, and extremely important, models. The 1500, 1600, 1800 and 2000 cars had quickly become profitable for BMW and, in true German tradition, this profit was reinvested in future products. It had become apparent that long-term survival was more likely by making a wider choice of cars over an equally wide price range. It's a policy that Volkswagen are keen to develop in the third millennium.

While the 1800 and 2000 remained in production to provide quick transport for well-heeled, middle-ranking 'executives', there was a new entry-level model – the 1600–2 – and a new flagship in the form of the attractively styled 2000CS Coupé.

THE 1600–2

In 1966 BMW celebrated its 60th anniversary as an engineering concern. It's an old cliché but valid nonetheless, that the 1600–2 (2 for 2-door) marked the beginning of a new era for the company, as this would project BMW on a long road to 'mega-stardom'. Already, BMW were eating hungrily into Daimler-Benz's share of Germany's increasing luxury car market.

With the 1600–2 that retailed in Germany at DM8,650 and in the United States at $2,680, it cost more than contemporary Fords and Opels, but it had a BMW badge. By 1966, thanks to the company's racing programme, this stood for a great deal, and customers queued endlessly at dealers' showrooms.

The car had been restyled and had a smaller, prettier and much leaner body, but was as well engineered as anything the company had made in the past. And its relatively low price was in no way reflective of cost-cutting exercises. The appearance of the new bodyshell had inevitable undertones of the 2000 but, with its steeply angled rear window – an attractive coupé touch – there was little doubt that the car was being aimed strongly at folks who might otherwise have gone for an Alfa.

The bodyshell was constructed in exactly the same way as the original 1500, but the 1600–2 had a 50mm shorter wheelbase, and held the distinct advantage from a performance point of view that the car weighed 100kg less than the 2000 model.

At the front were the chromed, kidney-style radiator grille – a long surviving feature of BMW's corporate image – two circular headlamps, an elegant bumper (with or without overriders) and wrap-around indicators below the bonnet line. Overall, the appearance was one of a rather friendly owl. Narrow bright mouldings were applied to the flanks at 'waist level', the roof rain channels, trailing edges of the rear lid and around the window glass.

Chromed hubcaps with BMW roundels at their centres were fitted to the smaller-diameter 13in steel wheels. Whitewall tyres were popular in North America, but found little favour in Britain or mainland Europe.

Debuted in the early 1960s the mid-range 1500 three-box saloon, although dogged by major teething troubles, rekindled BMW's fortunes.

A strong styling feature was the comparatively large circular tail-lamps. These had chromed bezels and an intriguing bright 'star' pattern to segregate the various functions. The star was an upside-down version of Daimler-Benz's famous motif, and sent an almost cryptic message to Stuttgart, that BMW was a now a real force with which to be reckoned.

No-Nonsense Cockpit

With two wide doors, access to the front or rear seats was excellent, and the glass area and slim roof pillars not only gave good all-round visibility, but a light, more modern feel to the interior. Such was the top quality of the fixtures and fittings, that it felt and looked like a Mercedes-Benz that had been on a severe diet for a long, long time.

Hard-wearing fluted vinyl was used for the seat upholstery and interior door and rear side panels. Slim, elegant bright mouldings were applied to the upper parts of the interior panelling, and a wider one ran across the redesigned dashboard. The steering wheel was again a rather inelegant and large two-spoker, and had an ugly rectilinear chromed horn ring that followed the contour of the spokes.

The dashboard layout was entirely functional, and although it wasn't austere in the Volkswagen sense, there was nothing particularly ornate about it. The three instruments – speedometer in the centre flanked by a fuel combination gauge on the left and clock on the right – were circular and positioned low down so as not to cast reflections in the windscreen. A generous-size glovebox sat in front of the passenger.

Road & Track's May 1967 road test described the interior as 'completely and satisfactorily finished off', and added:

> It isn't as rich in all details as the costlier BMWs but the materials are of good quality, in good taste, put together well; there's almost no resemblance to the almost naked appearance of most economy models. In many respects, such as having

the under-dash area neatly closed off by a padded panel, it puts many more expensive cars to shame ... Too many manufacturers save a penny in cost and lose a pound in quality. BMW hasn't.

Across the Bay

An overhead view of the engine compartment showed just what a well-thought-out little package the 1600 was. Not only was this 1,573cc (84mm bore × 71mm stroke) something of a gem in operation, it was also, like all BMW engines, very good-looking. The alloy box over the camshaft and rocker assembly was stamped proudly and prominently with the letters, BMW. It looked powerful merely sitting there doing nothing.

For economy a single Solex 38 PDSI carburettor sat below the massive, black-painted circular metal air filter. With a compression ratio of 8.6:1, reliability was assured and the engine, apart from being under-stressed, was capable of buzzing on regular premium fuels. In the good old days, when 99 Octanc 5-star petrol was available, these cars driven hard on a twisting road were almost unbeatable.

Developing a useful maximum 85bhp at 5,700rpm the car was capable of performing the 0–60mph sprint in just 11.4secs, and had a genuine top speed of 100mph. These were performance figures with which BMW almost shot themselves in the corporate foot; the 2000 Tilux, which cost nearly double the price of the 1600–2, was capable of a top speed of 110mph and, from 0–60mph, was only fractionally quicker at 10.5secs.

This went some way towards dispelling the long-held idea that, in the world of the automotive engineer, there was never a real substitute for cubic inches and horsepower. The real enemy of performance was excessive weight, as any lapsed athlete will confirm, and the 1600–2, while no match for its bigger brother in an out-and-out autobahn blast, was considerably more nimble

The 1600 saloon, developing just 3bhp more than the 1500, followed in 1964, but was overshadowed by the 1800 launched at the same time.

and 'chuckable' than the 2000 in the 'back lanes'. And this was just one reason why the press raved about it, and embarrassingly so for rival manufacturers.

Interestingly, many journalists felt compelled to compare BMWs with the Rover 2000TC which, with its 2-litre, single-overhead camshaft engine developing 124bhp, dependable road manners and graceful styling, was a similarly well-equipped motor car in the luxury 'quick' market.

It's an irony, though, that Rover, a once revered name in the industry, would eventually gain an unenvied reputation for a lack of reliability and poor build quality, before becoming a wholly owned subsidiary of BMW. Many journalists considered the Rover 2000TC to be a better car than the BMW, and said so in no uncertain terms between the hallowed covers of various respected journals, but it was BMW who would eventually win the day.

An interesting and amusing story that emerged from the BMW/Rover debate, was the one related by *Motor Sport*'s long-serving editor, Bill Boddy. At the end of 1969 the Bod, as he is affectionately known, was in line for a new company car and, all things considered, reckoned that the Rover 2000 saloon was about the best to cater for his motoring needs.

However, before taking delivery of his new car, Boddy telephoned his old chum Sam Clutton, the well-known Vintage Sports Car Club member and one-time owner of the Grand Prix Itala, to get an impression of Sam's views. Clutton had recently purchased a new Rover but had little to offer Boddy in the way of advice.

'What do you think of the Rover?' said Bill to Sam down a particularly crackly telephone line. 'Don't have any particular views about it, Boddy,' barked Clutton in his aristocratic manner, 'I've sent it back to Coventry so they can finish making it.'

This was something of an exaggeration, and intended partially as a joke but, as the recent history of the British motor industry has so transparently revealed, it was not particularly funny.

Of the BMW's power unit the writer of the *Autocar*'s June 1967 road test commented:

The reputation of the engine for smoothness is well founded, and this 1600 version is much sweeter than either the 1800 or the later 2000 with its stiffer crankcase. Camshaft whine seemed less on this test car than earlier ones, and we were able to run up to 50mph in second and 75mph in third without any effort at all.

'Flaw' on the Floor

The gearbox was to the same 4-speed synchromesh design as previous 'boxes with ratios as follows: First 3.84:1, Second 2.05:1, Third 1.34:1, Fourth 1:1, Final drive 4.11:1. There were mixed feelings as to how the unit felt in use. *Road & Track*'s testers omitted to make any notable comments, other than pointing out that they were able to shift gear at 6,000rpm as if they were the ones who were paying for the car, whereas the *Motor*'s staff were less convinced.

This English magazine's staff writer commented:

The fairly light, precise action for the gearchange was spoilt for some drivers by a large, knobbly plastic mushroom on top of the stout lever: frequent gearchanging could actually cause some soreness on the palm of the hand. Reverse gear, next door to first, could also be protected by a stronger spring to avoid the risk of wrong-slotting. Apart from these minority niggles, the gear lever is a pleasure to stir round the box. The realistic gearchange points on the speedometer – 26, 48 and 73mph –

With 90bhp in standard form the 1800 was among the quickest and best handling sports saloons of the mid-1960s. This model sold well despite keen competition from Rover, Triumph and to a lesser extent, Alfa Romeo.

correspond to 6,000rpm, 200 below the accepted limit although there is no rev counter to check the revs.

This same magazine in 1967 also noted briefly that the car was not fitted with a starting handle . . .

Handling, Riding, Stopping and Steering

The suspension system was to BMW's proven combination of MacPherson struts, wishbones, coil springs and telescopic dampers at the front, and semi-trailing arms, coil springs and telescopic shock absorbers at the rear. This gave the now predictable initial understeering handling characteristics, but journalists on both sides of the Atlantic – particularly the British – had reservations.

Whereas *Road & Track* pointed out that the generally excellent handling and stability had been achieved at the expense of ride comfort, *Motor*'s road testers were a little more scathing. The *Motor* even claimed that its drivers felt 'a little insecure in the car at first due to slight deadness in the medium-weight ZF worm and roller steering, and lack of lateral support offered by the front seats'.

The writer of the report acknowledged, however, that this feeling of insecurity was the result of hustling the car through corners at speeds which would have been nearly impossible in other makes of car. He wrote: 'On the slower corners the inside rear wheel can easily be spun and lifted, but bumpy roads have little effect on the cornering power.'

Whereas *Road & Track* were at pains to point out that 'Detroit wasn't in the same league when it came to combining ride and handling in the same suspension package,' *Motor* commented:

Perhaps the only feature of the BMW which falls below the high standard set by the rest of the car is the ride. This is firm and controlled, but there is some pitch and bounce on the sort of roughness to be found on the ordinary English country lanes and comfort is not as good in this respect as some of its rivals.

It is this author's contention that some English journalists had slightly misunderstood what BMW were getting at. This was a sporting machine that just happened to have a four-seater bodyshell, and it was natural in one sense that the BMW should be compared to other saloons, rather than sports cars with two seats.

Braking was taken care of by 9.5in-diameter discs at the front and 8in-diameter drums at the rear, noted by *Motor* after their usual 'abuse' test to be 'light, free of fade, but a little unprogressive'.

The only strange aspect of the car's make-up was that the battery, located on a shelf on the left-hand side of the engine bay, was a Bosch 6-volter. This held the advantage of being lighter in weight than a 12-volt unit, but was prone to suffer from voltage drop in cold weather, with the result that starting the engine could prove to be difficult or impossible. This was an oddity because the car was launched at the same time that the VW Beetle had switched from 6- to 12-volt electrics.

Except for the controversially styled headlamps, the 2000's body was the same as the previous model's. Between 1966 and 1972 these machines were perceived as the archetypal German middle-class conveyance – the German Rover 2000 – but are extremely rare today.

In Britain the car retailed at £1,298 including the much dreaded purchase tax which, for a performance 1600 capable of returning 30mpg, was attractively competitive. British concessionaires advertised the car widely under the banner: 'For the sheer joy of driving – unbeatable BMW.' This was a message that the company was keen to hammer home, and stuck rigidly to with similar slogans for many years. BMWs were all about driving and driving hard.

Politics

Behind the scenes in North America, there was something of a wrangle between *Car & Driver* and BMW's distributor, Max Hoffmann. One day in 1967 the Austrian telephoned the magazine's office to ask for an explanation as to why the latter had described the Rover 2000TC as 'the best sedan that we have ever tested.' Apparently he was labouring under the impression that Rover had exercised some kind of undue influence upon the magazine's testers to gain so much praise.

The reason for *Car & Driver*'s rave reviews of the British car was simply because the journal's writers considered it to be an excellent car, and also considered the BMW 1600 to be worthy of similar compliments.

Car & Driver's 1967 BMW 1600 road test writer remarked;

> To those who question as openly, as did Mr Hoffmann, we simply said that we would sing the praises of their products to the skies – if and when they managed to import something as good as the Rover, or better.

The report concluded in the following way, which pleased Mr Hoffmann:

> With the 1600, the consensus of our staff, and all our passengers, was that it looks, drives, feels, and sounds like it ought to cost at least a thousand dollars more. It also looks, drives, feels and sounds like it ought to kick the bejeezus out of the competition.

FLAGSHIP COUPÉ

During the 1950s and 1960s there was a noticeable trend among some manufacturers to imitate the successful products of rival car makers. This was, after all, one route to selling lots of cars, and this is why manufacturers are in business. The other path – a risky one in some cases – was to forge a more single-minded style in the hope that customers would like what they saw.

Today it is often said that Alfa-Romeo, who have launched several unusually styled cars, are right at the cutting edge of design. Love them or hate them, no-one can accuse the Italian firm of gaining inspiration from their competitors. This was the same for BMW when in 1965 the company launched its beautiful 2000C and 2000CS Coupé, styled in-house at Munich.

This was a significant model with a distinctive personality, that would be developed into something even more exciting, and was well received despite a hefty asking price – DM17,000 or $5,000 in North America. This was the luxury sports model that BMW had needed to fill the gap left by the 507 sports model which ceased production in 1959. It had taken some time but, by this stage, BMW could afford the luxury of producing a really top-notch touring machine.

To sell well, or sell at all, the car had to offer something over and above that which other cars, including Mercs, could give. That something was a uniquely styled bodyshell built by the old-established coachbuilding firm of Karmann based in Osnabrück. With its quad-headlamp layout, tall kidney grille

With its much neater body styling the 1600–2 was launched in 1966 and, as the company celebrated its 60th year as an engineering concern, marked the beginning of another era for BMW.

and clean-cut lines, the car resembled an aggressive shark from the front and, thanks to its slightly concave flanks, a lithe speed-boat from the rear.

A generously proportioned 2+2, with a larger rear seat than the 'plus two' appellation suggested, this was a Grand Touring motor car in the best tradition with comfort and equipment levels the equal of just about anything else around. In keeping with other models in the range, there was a large glass area, and chromed bumpers with rubber inserts and overriders, although the car looked better without either of the latter.

The use of bright trim was confined to the window perimeters, hubcaps and wheel trims, exhaust tail-pipe, mouldings along the flanks of the body at 'waist level' and along the leading edge of the front panel in front of the bonnet. In contrast to the circular headlamps, the tail-lamps were wide elongated pieces that partially wrapped around the outsides of the rear wings and were most attractive.

Some considered the front end to look really dismal, but stylist Wilhelm Hofmeister had pushed the boundaries to create an attractive-looking car without cutting corners. Attention to detail was marked and execution by Karmann was to their usual, high standards. The BMW badges at the base of the 'C' pillars, for example, concealed cabin ventilation outlets. Regrettably, a soft-top version was not on the cards, as tooling up for what was already a necessarily expensive machine would have been prohibitively expensive.

Interior Opulence

If the body styling was stunning, execution of the interior was no less so. The two fully adjustable Reutter front seats and rear bench were thickly padded, comfortably contoured and covered in the best quality fluted leatherette. A touch of individual style was added to this sumptuous interior by the huge chromed metal pieces that hinged the backrests of the front seats to the squabs. The interior panels were in similarly high-quality leatherette to match the seat covers, and generous bins were provided in the two doors for storing odds and ends.

The dashboard was completely new and significantly different from the other models in the range. *Road & Track* described the facia as a 'study in elegant simplicity', which was pretty accurate, and few owners disagreed. Extensive use was made of wood veneer for the facia, and padded leatherette covered the top surface below the windscreen.

Divided by a 'stepped' bar the lower portion contained the glovebox, heating and ventilation controls and steering column, while the upper segment comprised a wide, hooded instrument binnacle, circular fresh air vents and a radio speaker. The four circular instruments included an electric clock, speedometer, tachometer and a combination gauge on the right for fuel, water temperature, oil pressure, ignition failure and indicators.

Switchgear for the lights, windscreen wipers and heater blowers were neatly arranged in a row above the ventilation/heater controls in the centre, while the choke button was to the left of the steering column. Electrically operated door windows were available at extra cost, although the rear side windows were electrically controlled as standard. This arrangement was a little odd, but based on the idea that the driver couldn't be safely expected to control the rear windows while on the move. *Road & Track* commented:

Driver and passengers, then, are provided with luxurious, comfortable surroundings and the driver has good vision, instruments or warning lights, and major controls that facilitate a good command over the car's direction. The brake and clutch are too close to each other for bog feet, but the steering wheel, throttle and gear lever all seem to be in their right places.

The steering wheel was in the right place but, following contemporary German trends, it was again absurdly and unnecessarily large in diameter. Naturally, the floor was fully carpeted and rear legroom was surprisingly generous considering that the rear seat was intended for occasional use.

Like all well-engineered thoroughbred GT cars, the BMW cocooned driver and passengers from the outside world. The cabin felt like a safe, tranquil place to be, rather in the mould of a modern Jaguar or similar luxury car, and led a number of contemporary comentators to wonder how BMW could produce such a competent all-round package for the money.

Car & Driver's 1966 report commented:

The hardware is where the BMW really shines . . . literally. Its aesthetic appeal is that of a Bauhaus or Raymond Loewy award winning design. Everything operates with the precision of a key turning a Yale lock, and it's obviously built to outlast the tomb of Tutankhamen . . . Everything in the car is not only sturdy and well made, but thoughtfully laid out as well.

Pot Problems

In 1965 BMW had acquired a small but expanding parts bin, and the 1,970cc engine – also fitted to the 2000 saloon – had become a natural choice for slotting into the Coupé. The 2000CS manual gearbox version got the 'top-notch' 120bhp engine fitted with twin Solex 40PHH carburettors, whereas the 2000C automatic transmission car had the more 'cooking' 100bhp engine with a single Solex 40 PDSI carburettor.

The other fundamental difference between the two power units was the compression ratio – a high 9.3:1 for the manual transmission car and a safer 8.5:1 for the automatic. There was little doubt that this 4-cylinder overhead-camshaft unit was among the best power plants of its day, combining smoothly delivered power in abundant quantities.

Intellectually, however, it posed a problem for a car that was perceived and intended as a luxury Grand Tourer. At that time 2 litres was considered to be about the largest capacity that was practicably attainable with 4 cylinders. Plenty of manufacturers had produced 4-cylinder engines above this capacity, but they were harsh and unbalanced in operation. During the 1980s Porsche launched the 2.5-litre 944 4-cylinder car, but solved inherent vibration problems by placing counter-balancing weights on the crankshaft.

What BMW needed was a return to 6 cylinders, more horses and more cubic centimetres. These would eventually come, but the 2-litre 4-cylinder would have to suffice for the Coupé for the time being. While British and European customers were sympathetic, Americans well accustomed to 'monster' V8 engines, were less impressed. Despite modified, hemispherical combustion chambers for improved gas-flow and combustion, a top speed of 115mph and 0–60mph capability of 11.2secs – the automatic was good for 112mph – the engine was seen in North America as the car's weakest point.

Road & Track commented: 'It offers the same deficiency that most other European cars do, namely not enough displacement for adequate, effortless performance considering its price.' The report continued:

It idles smoothly and almost inaudibly at 700rpm, is fairly smooth at all constant speeds with no undue period effects, and is well enough sound-insulated from the interior so as not to intrude upon the generally low noise level at high road speeds. But it has to work hard for its living, is noisy on acceleration in the lower gears, depends upon the gearbox for its output, gives mediocre fuel economy and still can only manage modest performance in the 2600lb car. Nothing wrong here that an extra couple of cylinders and another liter of displacement wouldn't fix.

This was an understandable and typically American view, and BMW couldn't afford to ignore criticism of this kind, as North America was quickly becoming an increasingly important market. Europeans took a very different view and liked the engine's tractability, flexibility, acceleration through the gears and growling engine note above 5,500rpm. The tachometer, incidentally, was 'red-lined' at 6,500rpm with maximum power being developed at 5,800rpm.

Car & Driver's 1966 road test wasn't as scathing about the engine as *Road & Track*'s, and even bordered on being complimentary. The writer commented:

The torque and flexibility of the 2-liter engine suffice to keep the car lively in one gear lower or higher than the optimum for any given condition. It revs reluctantly above 5,000rpm, but there is more than enough punch from 1500rpm on up. In normal driving, there is no need to wind it up to its 6,500rpm maximum, but it's reassuring to have that margin there if you need a few extra moments of full power while passing a truck on the open highway.

One of BMW's major problems with which it had to deal was Porsche. The 911 model that made its debut in 1964 also had a 2-litre engine, but six, rather than four cylinders. Journalists and Porsche aficionados took the Zuffenhausen car to their hearts – they still do – and wrote rave reviews about it one after another. BMW wasn't strictly in the sports market, but there is no doubt that many customers who lusted after the inherent smoothness of a 6-cylinder engine were lost to Porsche. It was, however, good news for the Bavarian company, that Coupé owners loved everything, including the engine, about their cars.

Transmission

The same 4-speed Porsche-type synchro-mesh gearbox was used for the 2000CS as the saloon, and was inherently smooth and dependable. Bill Boddy of *Motor Sport* considered that it was only an 'abject fool who would object to Porsche's synchromesh gearbox'. Drive was through a 7.8in diameter clutch that required just 30lb of pressure at the pedal to operate. The gear ratios were as follows: First 3.835:1, Second 2.053:1, Third 1.345:1, Fourth 1:1, Final-drive ratio 3.90:1. The automatic version had ZF's 3-speed transmission and a 4.11:1 final-drive ratio to compensate for the lower powered engine.

According to some, the manual gearbox, with its light, positive throw, was one of the car's most appealing assets. Both up and down changes with the automatic gearboxes were hardly imperceptible by today's remarkable standards, but were good enough by comparison with other types from rival manufacturers.

Automatics were important at this stage for two quite distinct reasons. First, the majority of Americans preferred them. Second, women emerged in the 1960s as an independent force with much increased spending power, and women were buying and driving their own cars – a very different situation from the 1950s.

There was little, or no, evidence to suggest that the 'fairer sex' were not as competent at using a manual gearbox as their male counterparts, but this is certainly how some sectors of the motor industry perceived the situation.

If one of the 'chores' of driving had been taken away by the automatic gearbox, the unassisted steering was almost universally criticized for being heavy, particularly during parking manoeuvres and at low speeds.

Handling Package at No Extra Cost

In keeping with other models in the range, the big Coupé utilized MacPherson struts, lower wishbones, coil springs and an anti-roll bar at the front, and semi-trailing arms, large triangulated pieces mounted on a rubber-insulated sub-frame to reduce vibration, and coil springs at the rear.

Despite the car's weight, the handling characteristics were much what BMW owners had come to expect. On the standard crossplies – radials were available at extra cost – there was a discernible hint of initial understeer, turning to oversteer with hard application of the throttle, but always with the attitude of returning to the straight and narrow with less brutal treatment.

In reality it was a car, like its 6-cylinder successors, that demanded to be picked up by the scruff of the neck and booted hard, which is precisely how enthusiastic drivers dealt with their steeds. Conversely, it was always in fact quite difficult to get in the mood for booting a car, whose first effect on a driver was a feeling of safety and 'cocoonment' in the confines of a luxury cabin.

Even so *Car & Driver* commented:

Pressed hard, it lowers its nose like a bulldog; the tail rises slightly; the inside rear wheel starts to lift and the steering characteristic reaches oversteer just before breakaway. This is all done without deliberation and without any surprises. It would seem ponderous except that the car is getting around the corners much further than expected . . . Like previous BMWs, the 2000 is nearly fool-proof in a corner, and it is surprisingly easy to alter its direction when cornering, even when heavily committed to a line near the limit of adhesion. It's a car you just get into and drive, without any 'getting used to period'.

Ride quality was also excellent whether on smooth tarmac' or rough roads. *Road & Track* considered the suspension to be so good that driving over any surface should be part of the homework of all chassis engineers. This magazine's road tester commented:

Over the worst surfaces, with potholes, dips and humps, it's downright uncanny, for there doesn't seem to be an irregularity that can trip it up, even at twice the speed we'd dare go in a domestic sedan. 'But,' the Detroit engineers will tell you, 'you hardly ever dare drive on a bad road.' The fact is that we encounter enough rough road surfaces every day to appreciate this kind of suspension, and our driving conditions aren't typical.

This comment was pretty extraordinary because this was an American magazine, not just heaping huge quantities of glowing praise on the work of Munich engineers, but having a go at American car producers for not being able to compete. At this time, many American production saloon cars were in some respects somewhat agricultural by comparison with their European counterparts.

It was so often the case that they had a live rear axle suspended on leaf springs, with something of a 'soggily' coiled front end, which was fine on smooth road surfaces but akin to piloting a car ferry in a storm on rough ones. And there was another kind of drawback to this type of old-fashioned design; hit the brakes hard and the front end would feel as if it would bounce up and down for ever.

The BMW didn't feel anything like this. It was just the opposite. And its directional stability was also a huge improvement over US-grown products. This undoubtedly aided braking performance but, with 10.8in discs up front and the 9.8in rear drums, stopping performance was never much above adequate considering the engine's performance. What the car really needed was discs at the rear as well. The Rover 2000 had this arrangement and journalists, in comparing the two cars, came down in the British car's favour in this respect of the design.

A Minor Classic

Production of this model was dropped in 1968 to make way for the similar 6-cylinder 2800CS that had revised styling. Shortlived as it was, the 2000CS came to be regarded as a really special German motor car. Some regarded the frontal styling as catastrophically ugly and had the courage to say so.

European-spec cars differed markedly from the American-spec ones from the front. The former had an oval and circular headlamp cluster on each side shrouded by a piece of glass. This arrangement was actually illegal in the United States, where headlamps were compulsorily exposed, and

The 4-cylinder 2000 Coupé flagship debuted in 1965, the Karmann-built bodyshell providing a sound styling basis for the 6-cylinder 2800CS Coupé that went into production in 1968.

it was the US cars that came in for the most stick on the styling front as a result.

It was actually just an unconventional way of doing things on BMW's part, but reactionaries who were more used to a wide, chromed, gaping radiator grille, could see little merit in the aesthetics. Widespread criticism about the under-powered engine would have been stemmed a little if it had had twin overhead camshafts and 16 valves instead of the single overhead camshaft and eight valves. After all, the former had first seen service in the Ernst Henry-designed racing Peugeots as early as 1912, yet very few manufacturers took advantage of the design until the 1980s.

Despite all of this, it remains that the car was a quick, elegant and useful piece of touring machinery. By sticking religiously to 6,200rpm in acceleration tests, the 2000CS was capable of 28mph in bottom gear, 56mph in second, 90mph in third and 115mph in top.

LATE OPPOSITION

These figures may not make for exciting reading by comparison with modern BMWs, but they do compare especially well with, for example, the 'Droop Snoot' Vauxhall Firenza launched nearly 10 years after the 2000CS.

Like the BMW the Firenza was a four-seater coupé, fitted with a twin-carburettor 4-cylinder engine canted over at an angle. Developing 131bhp from 2,279cc, Bill Boddy of *Motor Sport* described the car a 'high performance four-seater'. Boddy's acceleration tests make for an interesting comparison with the BMW 2000CS. The Firenza's maximum speeds up through the gears were as follows; first 38mph, second 65mph, third 87mph, fourth 113mph, fifth 119mph.

With the benefit of ten years of development the Vauxhall was faster, but it also had a larger engine. Criticized for its difficult gearchange, lack of refinement and high interior noise levels, the Firenza was not a restful car to drive. On the other hand, the BMW was, and it was almost as quick.

Contemporary Alfas had comparable performance and equally good road manners, but Alfas were never as refined or as well built as the Munich car, and attracted a different, more sporting kind of driver. Volvo and Saab were building good, solid and reliable motor cars, but pedestrian performance indicated that both Scandinavian companies were heading for a different marketplace.

In the luxury saloon car market Daimler-Benz made peerless cars, although Jaguar and Rolls-Royce enthusiasts have usually agreed to differ on this point. By 1967 the motoring world had been virtually turned on its head. For the majority of manufacturers, increased standards demanded by the car-buying public required a much bigger march into the world of efficient mass-production.

The British luxury car manufacturer Alvis was in its death throes, BMC were in financial trouble as a result of an inability to rationalize its absurdly large range, while Ford, Opel and Volkswagen went from strength to strength. BMW were attempting to combine touches of the old world with the demands of the new one and succeeding admirably.

BMWs were beginning to appeal to, and be driven by, a different breed of people, who expected a great deal in exchange for their hard-earned cash. In conclusion to their 2000CS road test, *Road & Track* commented:

Whom is the new BMW for? It is for the person who values finish, detailing, finesse and integrity over pretense, excesses and sure obsolescence. It offers a unique combination of driver and passenger satisfaction, along with the promise of reliability and long life for which BMW cars are known, at a price in line with other such edifying cars. It may not have as much performance as we like, but we realize that no car near the price offers all that BMW has along with better performance – the rewards are worth the sacrifice.

Good as the 2000CS undoubtedly was BMW knew that it could be improved. The chassis was much too strong for the engine, and by 1968 the car was to provide the foundations of the visually similar 2800CS, a car that sent an immediate signal to Daimler-Benz's personnel, that they would soon be working rather longer hours in the foreseeable future.

4 2002 is Born: Realizing Perfection

GROWING UP

Evolution was gradually taking place in Munich. Quandt money had ensured that the company had been established on a firm footing, but no-one working on the factory floor, or in the boardroom, could afford the luxury of complacency. Lessons from the past had been well learnt, and the marketing department was beginning to understand more and more where the motoring world was heading.

Continued success of the company was dependent upon extreme vigilance, and keeping a constant eye on the various balance sheets. It was on this basis that BMW began to make the most of the parts bin, although American exhaust emissions legislation and safety regulations were to stretch the principles of BMW's engineers to some degree.

The pretty 1600–2 that made its debut in 1966 had created a huge impression on everyone who drove it. Quick, good-looking, beautifully screwed together, and with road manners that no other mid-range saloon could match, this model was just about classless. Sports cars like the MGB,

The 2002 appeared in 1968 and was hailed in many quarters as the definitive sports saloon. A 'giant killer', it was capable of running rings around traditional sports cars with much larger capacity engines.

Triumph Spitfire and Austin-Healey Sprite came a pretty poor second, but the British motor industry did nothing to stem the tide working against it.

BMW simply rubbed salt in the wounds of sports car fanciers by introducing the 2-litre engine to the 1600 bodyshell and sat back for reaction. Journalists enthused and never stopped. The vast majority pulled out all the stops in an attempt to express the view that, for the money, there was nothing to equal the 2002. Even when the 'value-for-money' Datsun 240Z sports car arrived in 1969, the Munich product continued in the eyes of journalists to be the car that had the most appeal to the discerning motorist.

The 2002 appeared in 1968, an intoxicating and euphoric period in the history of the motor car. In Italy, Ferrari launched two fabulous classics in the form of the Daytona 365 GTB and Dino 246, and Lamborghini were well under way with production of the V12 mid-engined Miura supercar. The latter not only stunned the world with its good looks and performance – and eventually its appalling reliability record – but was important as the first car to lead the way in doing away with copious quantities of bodywork bright trim. This lead would eventually have a heavy influence on other manufacturers including BMW.

The '02 appeared in different guises down the years, and included Cabriolet and Touring (Hatchback) versions. There were 2-litre, 1.8 and even a reversion to a 1.5-litre versions before production ended in the mid-1970s to make way for the 3 Series.

The 2002 was pitched into a fiercely competitive class that included Alfa-Romeo's Giulia twin-cam, Fiat's 125 twin-cam, the Vauxhall Victor and Ventura, Humber Sceptre, Sunbeam Rapier, the ever-present Rover 2000, Ford Corsair and

Taunus, Vauxhall Viva (Brabham and GT versions), and a host of mid-range saloons from Detroit.

And, of course, the Honda, Toyota, Datsun and Mazda names were beginning to make their presence felt by this time. In addition there were the Renault 16, Peugeot 404, Volvo 120 series, Cortina Lotus and the BMC 1800 'Landcrabs'. The manufacturers of these cars were all fighting with each other for a slice of the market.

For all its faults the revered magazine *Motor Sport* was widely acknowledged as a great source of independent wisdom. Editor Bill Boddy and continental correspondent Denis Jenkinson were usually amusing, sometimes bigoted, rarely wrong, often outspoken but always to be trusted for giving an honest view. In the February 1969 issue Boddy wrote:

> If I were asked, as I am asked, which is the most commendable car I tried in 1968 I would reply, without much hesitation, the BMW 2002. This was after my appetite had been whetted at a BMW party at the Wendover Club (and subsequently), but that is another story ... I discovered that I disliked the clutch action and rubber gear-lever knob of a BMW 1600, but I was able, later in the year, to drive more than 1,100 miles in a 2002. I have almost nothing but praise for this car and it did not have the 135bhp TI engine either.
>
> But the nice hundred horses it did have got this compact two-door saloon along effortlessly and endowed it with ample performance, if 93mph in third gear merits such comment. It handles pretty impeccably, like all the more recent BMWs, if functionally equipped, and accelerates in a hard purposeful manner. If one must criticize, the all-round independent suspension has a rather lively nature over rough roads.

This is precisely what BMW's staff wanted to know. They had done a great job. By contrast Boddy commented that he felt foolish in a Sunbeam Rapier fastback – 'like motoring to the Mansion House pretending to be a Le Mans winner.' He went on: 'Personal experience of a Jaguar 420T convinced me that I didn't want one, and I feel much the same about the much publicized, loudly proclaimed Jaguar XJ6 (which I have not yet driven) at all events until such time as this car has twice as many cylinders as at present.'

These were powerful words that became indelibly printed in the minds of *Motor Sport*'s many thousands of readers, and influenced future generations. One facet of road testing that Boddy had inherited from the post-vintage days before the outbreak of War was that of engine oil consumption. The table, reproduced here from the February 1969 issue of *Motor Sport*, makes comparison between various models. From a BMW enthusiast's point of view, they give fascinating insight.

Petrol and Oil Consumption of Cars Tested by the Editor in 1968

Car	*mpg*	*Oil thirst*
Opel Kadett	33.3	1 pint in 580 miles
Vauxhall Victor	24.9	4 pints in 740 miles
VW 1500 saloon	27.0	2 pints in 375 miles
Ford Escort GT	27.5	1 pint in 780 miles
Sunbeam Rapier	24.6	None in 350 miles
Rover 3500	19.0	
Roll-Royce	12.5	3 pints in 1335 miles
Mazda 1500 DL	31.1	2 pints in 1100 miles
VW 1600TL	26.2	None in 400 miles
Fiat 125	27.9	
Alfa Giulia Super	27.4	1 pint in 850 miles
Vauxhall Ventura	23.9	1 pint in 650 miles
Morris Minor	42.6	1 pint in 750 miles
Sunbeam Stiletto	37.1	0.5 pint in 700 miles
Reliant Scimitar	26.5	None in 650 miles
BMW 2002	30.8	0.5 pint in 1150 miles
Honda N360	44.5	None in 500 miles
Renault 16	26.2	0.25 pint in 670 miles
Gilbern Genie	18.7	1 pint in 645 miles
Cortina GT estate	30.0	None in 900 miles
NSU TT 1200	26.8	0.5 pint in 550 miles
Morgan plus 8	23.6	
Renault 16 TS	26.2	0.25 pint in 670 miles
Reliant Rebel	47.3	None in 450 miles
Morris 1800	23.0	
MG 1300	36.9	1.5 pints in 860 miles
Datsun 1600	29.1	None in 550 miles
Jensen FF	10.9	
Jensen Interceptor	14.5	None in 550 miles

Figures like these were studied avidly and digested wholeheartedly by *Motor Sport* readers, and foretold of the fortunes and misfortunes in store for the various manufacturers. It just so happened that the BMW 2002 made a huge impression. It was also an ideal weapon with which BMW could go motor racing in the European Saloon Car Championship, and at the same time attack sales markets throughout the world.

In the beginning there were two versions of the 2002. First the European-spec, or non-US version; this was fitted with the tried and tested 2-litre lump canted over at an angle of 30 degrees to allow for a low centre of gravity and low bonnet line. With a bore and stroke of 89×80mm, the capacity totalled 1,990cc. The compression ratio was relatively high at 9.3:1.

On twin Solex 40 PHH carburettors the unit developed 120bhp at 5,500rpm. The US version had a compression ratio of 8.5:1 and a single Solex 40 PDSI carburettor. This power unit developed 100bhp at 5,500rpm and was installed for the American market simply because the twin-carburettor version couldn't meet American exhaust emissions requirements. Both versions came with a choice of a 4- or 5-speed manual gearbox or automatic transmission. Ironically, the single carburettor 2002 produced little more power than the 1600 TI, but had an appreciable gain in torque – 97ft/lb at 4,500rpm for the 1600 and 116ft/lb at 3,000rpm for the 2002.

In powerful Tii guise the 2-litre 4-cylinder engine was capable of propelling the 'New Class' car, as BMW dubbed it, up to 125mph in roadgoing guise. Race-prepared engines were almost, but not quite, unbeatable.

The 2002's dynamics were so well thought out that it really was a car for all seasons, at home being hustled over a twisting Alpine pass, in its element on a racing circuit like the Nürburgring, and just plain suited to being pressed hard on a freeway.

Car & Driver's April 1968 road test was yet another bitter pill for Detroit to swallow. The writer of the report considered that buying anything other than a 2002 was a huge mistake for millions of Americans. In typically American contemporary style he commented:

In the suburbs, Biff Everykid and Kevin Acne and Marvin Sweatsock will press their fathers to buy HO Firebirds with tachometers mounted out near the horizon somewhere and enough power to light the city of Seattle, totally indifferent to the fact that they could fit more friends into a BMW in greater comfort and stop better and go round corners better and get about 29 times better gas mileage.

The mentality that stubbornly clung to the idea that a big engine was all that counted in a motor car was largely begun in America and, to a certain extent, prevails in that great country today. *Car & Driver* continued:

Mr and Mrs America will paste a 'Support Your Local Police' sticker on the back bumper of their new T-bird and run Old Glory up the radio antenna and never know that for about 2500 bucks less they could have gotten a car with legroom, more luggage space, good brakes, decent tires, independent rear suspension, a glovebox finished like the inside of an expensive overcoat and an ashtray that slides in and out like it was on the end of a butler's arm – not to mention a lot of other good stuff they didn't know they could get on an automobile, like doors that fit and seats that don't make you tired when you sit on them. So far as I'm concerned, to hell with all of 'em. If they're content to remain in the automobile dark, let them.

The 2002's interior was typically functional, with minimal instrumentation and an absurdly large steering wheel. This basic formula was little changed throughout the car's production run.

BMW 2000CS (1965–69)

Layout and Chassis	Unitary construction, all-steel two-door coupe

Engine

Type	In-line
Block material	Cast-iron with conventional water jackets
Head material	Light alloy
Cylinders	Four
Cooling	Water
Bore × stroke	89 × 80mm
Capacity	1,990cc
Valves	Two per cylinder
Timing	Single ohc
Compression ratio	9.3:1
Maximum power	120bhp at 5,500rpm
Maximum torque	123lb ft at 3,600rpm
Fuel system	Two Solex 40 PHH horizontal carburettors
Fuel tank capacity	16gal (73ltr)

Transmission

Gearbox	Synchromesh 4-speed manual with drive to the rear wheels through a conventional propshaft
Ratios	First 3.83
	Second 2.05
	Third 1.35
	Fourth 1.00
	Reverse 4.18
	Final drive 3.89
Clutch	Single dry-plate

Suspension and Steering

Front	Independent by MacPherson struts, coil springs and anti-roll bar
Rear	Independent by semi-trailing arms and coil springs
Steering	ZF Gemmer worm and peg with 3.3 turns from lock to lock
Tyres	175x14 radial
Wheels	Vented pressed steel 14inx5J

Brakes	Hydraulically operated discs (front), drums (rear)

Dimensions (in/mm)

Track	Front 52/1,330
	Rear 54/1,376
Wheelbase	100/2,550
Overall length	178/4,530
Overall width	66/1,675
Overall height	54/1,360
Dry weight	2,646lb (1,200kg)

Performance

Maximum speed	115mph (185km/h)
0–60mph (0–100km/h)	10.4sec
Standing quarter mile (0.4km)	17.7sec
Fuel consumption	15–24mpg (11.8–18.9ltr × 100km)

A superbly styled car by any standards, an original or well-restored 2002 still makes for a wonderful road car today. This example is fitted with modern BBS cross-spoke alloy wheels.

British enthusiasts dubbed the 2002 a 'giant killer', or wolf in sheep's clothing. Neither phrase was strictly accurate, particularly the latter, as the car's aesthetics were most unlike those of a sheep. In Germany the motoring journal *Auto Bild* coined the phrase *Flusten Bombe* – whispering bomb – which was not only spot-on, but held something of a ring of authority. And again readers took notice and reacted accordingly with their cheque books.

In some ways this was surprising because, during the mid-1960s, the German economy was plunged into temporary crisis. Like Britain in the 1980s Germany was in recession. Many parts of her motor industry were hit hard; there were redundancies, lay-offs and declining car sales. It was not a happy time but the BMW concern was an exception. During 1966–67 when even Volkswagen's board were running around like chickens with their heads removed looking for a suitable Beetle replacement, and Ford and Opel were looking up their collective bottoms to see if they still had

their hats on, BMW experienced a 34 per cent increase in sales. The company was, therefore, in a unique position.

Annual turnover had increased to DM820 million by comparison with less than DM200 million in 1963. At the end of 1968 turnover exceeded one billion marks. Interestingly, the motorcycle division of the company was also doing exceptionally well, despite (or because of) an out-of-date one-model design. Like the cars BMW motorcycles had a wide reputation in a number of countries for reliability, quality engineering and durability, and sales were undoubtedly aided by several of the world's police forces insisting on riding BMWs.

GLOBAL COMMITMENT

It was at this time that the company's distribution and technical service department was expanded and improved. The dealer network was expanded at the same time in the same way that Volkswagen's had been some years previously. BMW's top executives constantly made long trips abroad that resulted in the setting up of offices in Austria, France, the Netherlands, Switzerland, Belgium, Britain, the United States and Finland. Yugoslavia, Bulgaria and Hungary, countries which at that time were still Communist controlled and behind the Iron Curtain, were also eventually added. An assembly plant was also established in South Africa.

Such was the success of the company that it also started on plans for new headquarters at Munich. This was a multi-million-mark building – the famous 'cylinder' tower block – that students of architecture the world over would marvel at.

The skills of the marketing men were clearly not at variance with those of the engineers who had created the 2002. Perceptions of both the company and cars changed markedly with this model, and it was against a thriving background, that owners and journalists banged on constantly about the car's merits and apparent lack of faults.

In the Old Mould

The 2002 was a mid-range saloon of the New Class, as BMW had dubbed it, made up of many thousands of parts. Individually, there was nothing particularly stunning about any of the components, but there is no doubt that, taken as a whole, the sum of these parts amounted to a classic sports saloon in the pre-War 328 guise.

Bodily the car was no different from the 1600, apart from the badging on the rear panel proclaiming a larger engine under the front lid. At 2,210lb the 2002 weighed some 160lb more than the 1600 but, with a larger engine and a 27 per cent gain in torque, the weight penalty was insignificant from a driver's point of view.

The '02 series cars form the backbone of today's thriving BMW classic movement, and continue to draw interest at club events.

With bodyshells by Baur of Stuttgart, the 1600–2 Cabriolet joined the range in 1967. Fitted with the 1600 engine initially, these wonderful cars developed 85bhp and were easily capable of 95mph.

Function and Form

The interior was also similar to the 1600's, with the same facia layout and large-diameter 3-spoke steering wheel. The instrument cluster was styled without much in the way of artistic imagination, but the gauges were crystal clear and easy to read. They comprised a fuel combination gauge on the left, a speedometer in the centre and clock on the right. Major switchgear was positioned left and right of the instrument binnacle with symbols on each to indicate their function.

Surprisingly, the various knobs were not 'flattened' off in the interests of passenger safety. This went against the grain of contemporary thinking and was certainly against Ralph Nader's sense of automotive decorum. We can only speculate that BMW's designers had their own good reasons for this apparent oversight. The most likely argument is that a driver who, in the event of an accident, made contact with the knobs was likely to be beyond help anyhow, having probably encountered the steering wheel at high speed first.

The upper part of the dashboard was covered in a padded and non-reflective material, and separated from the lower surface by a stepped bar. High-quality vinyl was used to cover the seats and interior panelling, and the front seats were fully adjustable and reclined, but head restraints were extra-cost options.

Car & Driver's road tester was interested in exactly whom the 2002 would appeal to and commented:

> I'll be interested to see who those 10,000 owners of the 1968 BMW 2002 actually turn out to be. The twits won't buy it, because it's too sensible, too comfortable, too easy to live with. The kids won't buy it because it doesn't look like something on its way to a soft moon-landing and it doesn't have three billion horsepower. BMW buyers will – I suspect – have to be pretty well adjusted enthusiasts who want a good car, people with a sense of humour to enjoy its giant-killing performance and the taste to appreciate its mechanical excellence.

Round the Bend

To improve the car's handling and road-holding capabilities, which was necessary in view of its gain in weight over the 1600 version, BMW fitted much stiffer suspension. The layout was the same – MacPherson struts, lower wishbones and (optional) anti-roll bar at the front, and semi-trailing arms and coil springs at the rear.

Many of the car's cornering characteristics could be attributed to the stiff and rigid bodyshell, an inherent facet of all really well-constructed two-door cars. With a horizontal roll axis and precise, direct steering, the 2002 'sang' through the corners safely at high speed on an even keel with all but the most unforgiving drivers at the wheel.

Crossply tyres were standard wear in most markets, although 13in Michelin XAS radials were available as extra-cost options, and owners who despaired with the former (the majority), quickly switched to the latter. Typically, the car understeered at the limit, as the weight of the engine was concentrated in the nose. Taken beyond the limit, a rear wheel had a tendency to cock itself in the air, but the speed at which this usually occurred was not something BMW sought to encourage on public roads.

Road & Track commented:

> In normal fast driving the driver will never encounter wheel lift and he'll find himself covering the ground rapidly, no matter what the surface. This wheel lift and the BMW characteristic of violent wheel hop when 'popping' the clutch for acceleration runs, are apparently the results of very light shock control, which does not, however, create a sloppy ride.

With so much engine torque spread evenly across the rev range the 2002 was hardly a car that needed its gearbox stirring on a regular basis, but banging the lever up and down was always a riot of fun, which is why the people who enjoyed their driving tended to do this more often than was strictly necessary. The extensive use of rubber bushing in the gear linkage ensured that changes were always smooth.

Driving through a 7.9in single dry-plate clutch, the gear ratios differed from the 1600's and are as follows: First 3.84:1, Second 2.05:1, Third 1.35:1, Fourth 1:1.

A SPECIAL

Until the advent of the 2002 turbo version in 1973, the most desirable and powerful version of the car was produced by the German tuning company, Alpina. Alpina have been 'breathing' heavily on BMWs for many years, always with astonishing results, but their tuned 2-litre was their first attempt at making a true 'nutter's Q car'. It happened in 1967.

Alpina took a 1600 version, installed the 2000 TI engine, went to work and produced a car that, in some respects, was better than BMW's own 2002. It went like stink! In place of the stock 40mm Solex carburet-tors, there was a brace of 45mm twin-choke Webers, the compression ratio was raised from 9.3:1 to 10.5:1, and power output was usefully increased from 135bhp to 160bhp.

By German standards, the Cabriolet's soft-top was rudimentary, but kept out the elements well enough.

Later Cabriolets had a 'roll hoop' at the rear to protect passengers in the unfortunate event of inversion. This did little to enhance the car's styling but successfully appeased the demands of safety-conscious Americans.

With Alpina's customary attention to detail, the standard 4-speed gearbox was changed for a close-ratio 5-speeder, a limited-slip differential was installed and the final-drive ratio was changed from 4.11:1 to 3.89:1. Michelin XAS radial tyres were fitted as standard and, in conjunction with vented front brake discs, the car had sensational stopping power.

Suspension modifications included stiff Koni shock absorbers (adjustable at the rear) and springs, and stiffer anti-roll bars at both ends. The steering ratio was also altered from 17.6:1 to 12.8:1. Externally, the car was distinguishable from the standard range by Alpina badges on the front wings, but, curiously, a 1600 badge was left in place on the rump below the bootlid.

Inside the car there were Recaro sports seats, a leather-trimmed steering wheel with three 'drilled' alloy spokes to a revised design, and a tachometer 'red-lined' to 7,200rpm in place of the standard clock. it was odd that manufacturers, and BMW were no exception, considered a clock to be so necessary. After all, the majority of people at this time could get the same information from the instrument that most wore on their wrists. So, full marks to Alpina for fitting a tachometer!

Mighty Machine

By any standards the Alpina BMW was a formidable piece of equipment. It was also as expensive to buy as a Porsche 911. Its appeal, therefore, was strictly limited to impecunious dreamers, and well-heeled fanciers of a genuine 'Q-craft'. What Alpina had created was a genuine 'pocket-rocket' with rarely equalled performance.

Arguably the world's first 'hot hatchback', the three-door Touring version was launched in 1971. Engines ranged from 1600 to 2 litres.

There were plenty of 'supercars' around at this time, which had higher top speeds, but few were able to sit on the Alpina's tail on a twisty road. When it was launched few people had ever seen anything like it. In Britain a performance saloon was measured by the dynamics of the Rover 2000TC. By comparison with the Alpina BMW it was a slothful sluggard. Not even contemporary Alfas were in the same performance league, and Triumphs, MGs, Austin-Healeys and so on simply didn't get a look in.

The BMW would typically accelerate from 0–60mph in 8.3secs, 0–100mph in 20secs and perform the standing quarter-mile in 15.7secs. Top speed worked out at around 125mph but, as usual, such performance came at the expense of hefty fuel consumption. Between 15–17mpg was typical, and many customers plumped for the optional 19.8-gallon fuel tank (double the capacity of the standard car's), which gave a useful range of up to 360 miles.

Using a maximum of 7,200rpm through the gears this car would reach 38mph in bottom gear, 59mph in second, 82mph in third, 101mph in fourth and 125mph in top, performance which was well beyond anything in the 2-litre class in the mid-1960s. In fact, these figures are similar to those expected of performance 2-litres in the 1990s.

Almost without exception, contemporary road testers criticized the sloppy and remote gear linkage and the consequently 'rubbery' feel this gave when gear changing but, in all other respects, the car was apparently vice-free. In many ways the Alpina provided an ideal rally car for privateers. The car's strength, handling and performance was far in advance of even works efforts from Ford, Lancia and Saab, and would even have given the 2-litre 911 Porsche a good run for its money. But, alas, few privateers could afford the expense of buying one of these exemplary machines, let alone enter one in the rough and tumble of competition.

An all-time classic, these cars are rare today and much coveted by BMW aficionados.

TOPLESS TEUTON

From 1967 the so-called New Class range included an attractive Cabriolet, designed and built to broaden the range's appeal to younger drivers. Built by the Stuttgart body-making firm, Baur, these cars originally came in 1600 form, developed 85bhp and had a top speed in the region of 95mph.

Some 4,000 were made up until 1975 when production ended, but a BMW 'ragtop' was always going to be destined for relatively low production volume. The same body style was retained, of course, but was substantially strengthened internally to compensate for the loss of torsional rigidity in having had its roof 'removed'. As a result it was substantially heavier than the regular saloon, but this extra weight had little effect on overall performance.

A most elegant looking car, and fun to drive, the first series Cabriolets had a fully reclining, fold-away soft-top, secured to the top of the windscreen frame at the front with a catch on either side. In the down position this long 'sandwich' structure folded away behind the rear seat, and was closed with a 'boot', or cover, that clipped with 'poppers' located on the rear scuttle.

Four-seater Cabriolets were relatively rare, but German engineers had never been afraid to exploit this part of the niche market. Pre-War 'monsters', the likes of Horch and Daimler-Benz, demonstrated perfectly, that German engineering integrity ensured that the long-wheelbase convertibles were strong and safe. They were also expensive, but this doesn't fully

Wind-tunnel tests demonstrated that the Touring, with its sloping tailgate and Kamm tail, was aerodynamically superior to the regular 2002. On the road it felt as taut and agile as any other Bee-em of this period.

Although expensive to buy the 1600 Touring made for competent, sporting family transport. Developing 85bhp this car wasn't a match for the later 1.6-litre Volkswagen Golf GTi, but it was a fair effort for the early 1970s.

explain why so relatively few examples were produced.

According to post-War German and British motoring lore, a 'proper' driver's car had an integral roof panel. Soft-tops were for those who didn't take the business of hard driving seriously. This feeling was particularly prevalent among the Porsche fraternity, who traditionally looked down their noses at the Cabriolet versions of the 356. Cabriolets were only rarely as aerodynamically efficient as 'tin-tops' – with the soft-top down at any rate – and it is for this reason that the majority chose to drive a 'proper' car. BMW's customers were no exception to this general rule.

The Cabriolet was not, therefore, to be taken too seriously, even in its later 2-litre form, but it did provide 'flies-in-the-throat' enthusiasts with welcome fresh-air motoring in the hot summers characteristic of the central European continent and California.

Making a Point

In characteristic German fashion BMW made no extravagant claims about this, or any of their other, models. The company's publicity literature was brief, concise and to the point:

A sporting car, quick and agile. Safe and reliable. Spirited and superior like the sedan. But with a top that can be opened. Sporty driving, top-down driving – for many the two belong together. For the convertible owner, the joy of driving is paramount. All the better, the BMW Cabriolet has the same performance and safety reserves as any BMW.

This is how BMW saw its products on the world stage. There was little doubting the car's superiority and engineering prowess, even if many secretly boiled in annoyance at such a seemingly arrogant attitude. Nonetheless, it was true, which is why BMW would go on in future years to produce the 'ultimate driving experience' and so many others would not.

In 1971, the Cabriolet's bodyshell was substantially revised to include a roll-over hoop, with a small integral window on each side behind the door windows. This wasn't a Cabriolet in the true sense, but more of a 'targa top' along the lines of the Triumph Stag and the Targa version of Porsche's 911. The car came with the 2-litre engine and was badged as a 2002 but, for all its increased performance and excellent road manners, it looked awkward by comparison with its handsome predecessor.

This was inevitably an attempted compromise on the part of the designers to make a car that had the inherent strength and safety of a saloon, but with the fresh-air advantages of a full convertible. The soft-top was made in two pieces, namely a removable piece above the front compartment, which could be stowed in the boot, and a rear section containing the plastic rear window. The latter folded down in the normal manner of a soft-top, and was closed with a tonneau cover that clipped to the bulkhead.

The roll bar over the cockpit was massively strong, and well capable of remaining intact in the unfortunate event of the car turning turtle, but it was hardly satisfactory from an aesthetic viewpoint. However, these cars were built during the 'hysterical' Nader era. In recent times, of course, BMW's Cabriolets and open-top sports cars have reverted to the original design of 1967, in that they have no roll-over hoop. The windscreen pillars are sufficiently strong in themselves not to warrant an additional roll hoop.

THE FIRST 'HOT-HATCHBACK'

Volkswagen enthusiasts vociferously contend that the VW Golf GTi was the first true 'hot hatch'. Students of British motor manufacturing have always been keen to point out that the Farina designed Austin A40 was the first hatchback, but this car was far from hot, even by the standards of the late 1950s and early 1960s.

Launched in 1971 the Touring version of the New Class car was arguably the first truly 'hot' hatchback, preceding the Golf GTi by several years. The Touring, or estate, version was an addition to the range and never intended as a replacement for the standard saloon.

Fundamentally, it was the same car as the 2002, but with freshly designed hind quarters. The 'C' pillars, containing fresh-air grilles, sloped steeply down to the back of the rear wing and a large third door, supported in the up position by a strut on each side, replaced the more normal bootlid. At first glance this gave little advantage over the more conventional three-box saloon, but BMW's masterstroke lay in dividing the rear seat to fold down in separate parts.

This increased the cargo volume considerably, and led to a new way in which designers thought about medium-size saloons in Europe. The car started what *Motor Sport*'s long-standing continental correspondent referred to as the 'Eurobox' phenomenon. 'Jenks' criticized such cars out of hand, often citing them as 'super shopping trolleys' on the one hand, while begrudgingly admitting on the other that they were capable of running rings around the out-and-out sports cars of just a decade before.

The Touring was available as a 1602, 1802, and 2002 with all variants – carburettor and fuel injection – on each. Some

32,000 examples were made all told, which clearly indicated that BMW were not, even at this stage, attempting to compete with big volume producers like Volkswagen.

Red Enemy

In the company's publicity literature, BMW made a point that these cars were well protected against corrosion. A new painting and sealing process had been introduced that 'prevents corrosion before it can occur'. In the early 1970s manufacturers began to tackle 'tinworm' seriously for the first time. Car buyers were well and truly fed up with having to deal with unsightly patches of body rust, particularly along the bottoms of the doors and around the wheel arches, but early methods of rust inhibition were crude; the passage of time has demonstrated that these cars corroded badly, as there are so few survivors.

An Interesting Exercise

Wind-tunnel designed and tested, the Touring held aerodynamic advantages over and above the regular saloon. With the sloping tailgate and Kamm tail, air running over the top of the car was more cleanly dispersed, a facet of the design that was confirmed by Volvo in the mid-1990s when the Swedish company ran its estate cars, in place of its saloons, in the British Touring Car Championship.

In its 2002 Tii 2-litre format the car developed the usual 130bhp – the same engine fitted to the 2000 saloon – but this fuel-injected version was not exported to the United States. Again, it was incapable of meeting exhaust emissions regulations, and the Americans had to settle for the single carburettor 2-litre 113bhp engine.

Logically, of course, the Touring should have been badged as a 2003. After all, the

2002 was so called to avoid confusion with the 2000, but 'Touring' was considered more appropriate, and it's a name that has been used for BMW's estate cars ever since. In producing this and the big 6-cylinder cars, BMW were heavily engaged in trendsetting. Their example was both followed and copied by others.

During the late 1960s and early 1970s, Britain had nothing directly comparable to BMW's Touring, although some hailed the five-door Austin Maxi as a car of similar design thinking. To have compared the Maxi with the BMW was foolish. The two cars were miles apart in almost every respect, the former eventually becoming something of an embarrassment.

In February 1970 Bill Boddy writing in *Motor Sport* commented:

I drove away in the Austin Maxi with hope in my heart that this would be the breakthrough that the British Motor Industry so badly needs. It had a clever five-door body in its favour but I have to admit, like other critics, that the Maxi was too noisy, lacked power unless the revs were kept well up, had a notchy cable-actuated gear-change, and that its five-speed gearbox was really an alternative to having over-drive and that its rack and pinion steering was too low geared, especially on its too upright column.

Boddy went on:

The overhead camshaft 1.5-litre engine was new but also outdated, being of iron, with a chain-driven o.h. camshaft for its non-crossflow head. I tried hard to like this new BMC car and it does have the secure road-clinging and handleability for which the Issigonis/Moulton suspension formula is renowned. But this didn't add up, in total, as a brilliant new 1969 offering; I say this with regret.

Like the contemporary 2-litre Volvo 145S estate, the BMW Touring cost over £2,000 in Britain and had a maximum speed of 106mph, but felt a whole lot better from behind the wheel.

This was a sad, but accurate, picture of Britain's motor industry. Ford were making acceptably good cars but they weren't in BMW's street for quality or performance. Just two years earlier Bill Boddy had described the 2002 as the best of the bunch of cars he'd driven in 1968 – it was he remarked 'a gentleman's saloon'. At the time of the Austin Maxi's launch nothing happened to reverse the editor of *Motor Sport*'s respected opinion.

MID-LIFE CRISIS

Without exception German manufacturers have never indulged in the fruitless and irritating habit of launching new models at frequent intervals to appeal to the unfounded whims of marketing people. Salesmen working in dealer networks become bored as a result of seeing the same style cars day in day out, but this is hardly a good reason for manufacturers to rush off and retool for a new machine.

BMW felt the same way about the New Class '02s but, by the early 1970s, journalists were starting to make noises that these cars were beginning to look a little long in the tooth. BMW responded in 1971 with a 'facelift' for the range. In the United States the 1602 and 1802 were dropped altogether, this market being treated solely to the standard 2002 and 2002 Tii. In America the cars had safety reflectors on the sides of the front and rear wings, larger bumpers with heavy rubber inserts and a rubber moulding running the length of the body's flanks.

This latter change was not uncommon in the 1970s; it was a means of protecting body and paintwork in tight car parking spaces, but a practice that has been dropped in recent times on aesthetic grounds. In the cabin the front seats were re-contoured to enhance comfort, and the instruments were redesigned to give a crisper, fresher appearance.

BACK IN THE US-OF-A

The Americans were particularly pleased at this time because, at long last, the 2002 Tii with Kugelfischer mechanical fuel injection became available. It had finally made its way through the stringent emissions tests but, to do so, the compression ratio had been lowered from 10:1 to 9:1. The engine developed a maximum 140bhp at 5,800rpm, the car boasted a top speed of 118mph and could reach the benchmark 60mph figure through the gears in 9.8secs. 100mph from rest took no more than 32secs. There was 145lb/ft of torque at 4,500rpm. Around 23mpg could be expected as an average and, with its 12.1-gallon fuel tank, there was a range of approximately 280 miles.

In standard form the car was fitted with 4-speed manual transmission by Borg-Warner, rather than the Porsche synchromesh system as previously, and the ratios were as follows; First 3.76:1, Second 2.02:1, Third 1.32:1, Fourth 1:1, Final-drive 3.45:1. A 5-speed ZF gearbox was available at extra cost and had a final-drive ratio of 4.11:1. The move from the Porsche synchromesh gearbox was almost undoubtedly prompted by continuous criticism about the sloppy, soggy feeling to the shift.

Road & Track's journalists were more than happy with this version of the 2002. The writer of the 1971 test report remarked:

In all the 2002 Tii offers a good combination of performance, refinement and economy, and our only serious question is about the gearing. The gearbox itself is a delight, with a wonderfully smooth synchronizer action of just slight notchiness as one moves from

Later Tourings had more generously ventilated road wheels without trims, which led to much improved brake cooling.

gear to gear offering a feel of precision rather than real resistance.

What really made the BMW worthwhile for this magazine's staff was its responsive engine, nice gearbox and good controls. It was, they proclaimed, a real driver's machine. Apart from the gearing, criticism was confined to the lack of air-conditioning – an almost mandatory requirement in America – and relatively poor ventilation system.

Germans had never been particularly thoughtful over the design of fresh-air systems, which was probably the quite understandable result of suffering ice-cold blasts of air from the mountains of Switzerland during Bavarian winters, and few can blame them for this. Bavaria in winter is cold!

The Tii had wider 5in wheels and stiffer suspension than the standard 2002, which improved roadholding to cope with additional engine power, but this was clearly a compromised set-up. On the one hand, this was a relatively heavy saloon; it demanded stiff suspension but, unlike so many sports saloons, ride quality remained smooth and comfortable over irregularities in the road surface.

R&T's RIVAL MACHINES

Road & Track made an interesting comparison with BMW's nearest rivals, the Alfa-Romeo 1750 Berlina and Volvo 142E. All retailed in the United States at around $4,000. Of the three, the BMW was the lightest car at 2310lb and the Volvo the heaviest at 2696lb.

In the 0–60mph dash the BMW proved fastest at 9.8secs, the Volvo scored a creditable 10.5secs and the Alfa a surprisingly pedestrian 11secs. Over the standing quarter-mile the 2002 managed a run of 17.3secs, the Volvo 17.5secs and the Alfa 17.9secs. Fuel economy discrepancies were interesting too, the Volvo winning all hands down with an average of 23.7mpg, the 2002 slightly behind at 22.7mpg and the Alfa scoring badly with just 20.4mpg.

On their own these statistics are fairly meaningless, although many took notice of them when it came to buying a car costing $4,000. From the point of view of someone who took real pride in his or her ability to get the most from a sports saloon, the most telling statistics were those relating to the cars' cornering abilities.

Road & Track's staff took the considerable trouble to record the cornering capability in terms of G-forces working against each of these vehicles, and discovered that the BMW was well in advance of the Alfa and the Volvo. The figures were 0.726, 0.692 and 0.649 respectively, and provided a truer picture of the kind of design thinking that prevailed at Munich.

Producing a fast, comfortable four-seater was easy – Detroit had been doing it for years – but striving to build a car that had the advantage in almost all aspects of design was at the cutting edge.

Road & Track concluded that the 2002 Tii was a

real blast to drive fast and yet practical enough for a small family to use for daily transportation and extended trips ... The price is high and getting higher, thanks to the German currency's upward spiral, but the 2002 Tii is bound to give BMW's little 2-door a popularity boost. It certainly gives our collective mood a boost – it's nice to know that even with tightening smog regulations it's possible to get more performance in a car that was already strong in that department.

The controversial 2002 turbo – killed off by the oil crisis in 1973 – paved the way for other manufacturers, including Saab and Renault, to adopt forced induction as a relatively simple route to increased engine power. Developing 170bhp at 5,800rpm, this BMW was capable of 135mph.

Arguably the most coveted and collectable of the '02 range, turbos are easily capable of keeping pace with modern performance BMWs.

PRESSING ON

In 1972 production of the aged 2000 and 1800 saloons finally came to an end. The 2-litre car had enjoyed a relatively successful production run, with 143,464 units having been sold all told. By comparison with the '02 range, these cars were great lumbering machines with out-of-date styling. They had had their day and BMW were grateful, but the company continued to project its sporting image.

The company knew exactly where it was going, what it wanted, and more important, what its customers required. Taking part in international competition had by this stage become an important part of the company's marketing strategy. Famous names like Hans-Joachim Stuck had been brought in to drive the 6-cylinder CS Coupés in track racing events, which served as one means of explaining to the car-buying public, that Munich made cars the equal of anything being produced in Stuttgart by Daimler-Benz and Porsche.

BMWs were exciting to drive, exciting to look at, and in both respects were part-way between the Mercs and Porsches. But BMW always had another trick up its sleeve. In 1973 the company launched the ultimate roadgoing 2002 – the turbo. This, although a victim of circumstance, would ultimately influence the motoring world for the foreseeable future.

TURBO AND TROUBLE

Unveiled to the public at the Frankfurt Motor Show in September 1973, the 2002 turbo proved to be something of a shock to those who had considered the Tii to be the last word in 4-cylinder sporting saloons. This was a 'milestone' car in that it was the world's first production car with a turbocharged engine.

It didn't, however, meet with universal approval. Upon its launch some journalists – mostly from Germany – objected to its aggressive looks. They also criticized the turbo lettering on the front chin spoiler, which was written backwards and would only read correctly, when viewed by motorists in their rear-view mirrors.

This, some claimed, was provocative and encouraged drivers to conduct their cars at excessive speed, although few actually defined what excessive speed was. Such folks were quickly named as 'nannies' by the popular press, and they've been with us ever since.

The BMW turbo, like so many other cars fitted with these power-enhancing devices, suffered from several problems, which is why, a quarter of a century after BMW pioneered their use, they are almost obsolete in all but diesel-engine applications. High under-bonnet temperatures, heavy fuel consumption, poor longevity, throttle 'lag' and the sheer expense of maintenance were all part of the turbo package, and manufacturers seeking to produce more power 'artificially', would eventually rediscover and perfect the art of supercharging.

Delving Deep

With the BMW turbo, the first problem that had to be solved before it was let loose on the public, was the frequency with which the exhaust manifolds cracked. This was as a result of it having to cope with exhaust gases that it fed to the turbocharger at an uncomfortably high temperature of 1,650 degrees F.

BMW had a rethink and made the manifold with a high nickel content, that proved to be more satisfactory than the standard 2002's pure cast-iron unit. The turbocharger itself – a German-made KKK item – was neatly installed under the front lid, driven by exhaust gases and blew fresh air to the inlet manifold through a pipe. A throttle valve designed to open when boost reached 8psi was situated in the pipe between the

Although relatively expensive to prepare, the 2002 provides 'clubbie' racers with a competitive machine in modern events.

BMW 2002 (1968–75)

Layout and Chassis Unitary construction, two-door saloon

Engine
Type	In-line
Block material	Cast-iron with conventional water jackets
Head material	Light alloy
Cylinders	Four
Bore × stroke	89 × 80mm
Capacity	1,990cc
Valves	Two per cyliunder
Timing	Single ohc
Compression ratio	8.5:1
Maximum power	100bhp at 5,500rpm
Maximum torque	115ft lb at 3,000rpm
Fuel system	Single Solex 40PDSI carburettor
Fuel tank capacity	12.1gal (55ltr)

Transmission
Gearbox	Manual 4-speed synchromesh, or 3-speed automatic
Ratios	First 3.84
	Second 2.05
	Third 1.35
	Fourth 1.00
	Final drive 3.64
Clutch	Single dry-plate

Suspension and steering
Front	Independent by MacPherson struts, coil, springs and anti-roll bar
Rear	Independent by semi-trailing arms, coil springs and anti-roll bar
Steering	Worm and roller with 3.75 turns lock to lock
Tyres	Michelin 165HR13 XAS radial
Wheels	Pressed steel vented 13inx4.5in

Brakes Power assisted discs (front), drums (rear)

Dimensions (in/mm)
Track	Front 52/1,330
	Rear 52/1,330
Wheelbase	98/2,500
Overall length	167/4,230
Overall width	63/1,590
Overall height	56/1,410
Dry weight	2,183lb (990kg)

Performance
Maximum speed	111mph (179km/h)
0–60mph (0–100km/h)	9.7sec
Standing quarter mile (0.4km)	17.4sec
Fuel consumption	20–25mpg (11.3–14.2ltr × 100km)

For variations relating to the 1602, 1802 and 2002Tii , see the main text. Utilizing the same basic engine as the 2002, the turbo model (1973–74) produced 170bhp at 5,800rpm with a compression ratio of 6.9:1 and Kugelfischer PL04 fuel injection and KKK BLD turbocharger. Top speed of the turbo was in the region of 130mph (209km/h) and the car was capable of accelerating from 0–60mph in 6.7sec.

turbo and exhaust manifold. It was a magnificently simple interpretation of early turbocharging, but at this stage the system did not include the all-important inter-cooler.

Apart from altered ignition timing, lower compression ratio of 6.9:1 and an additional oil cooler, the engine was a standard 2002 Tii unit, but one that developed 170bhp at 5,800rpm and 179lb/ft of torque at 4,000rpm. Schafer mechanical fuel injection was employed instead of the more normal Kugelfischer, and in standard form, power was fed to the rear wheels through a manual 4-speed gearbox. The gear ratios were as follows: First 3.35:1, Second 1.86:1, Third 1.28:1, Fourth 1:1, Final-drive ratio 3.36:1. A 5-speed manual gearbox was available at extra cost.

A Racer Explains

Winner of the 1961 Le Mans 24 Hours in a Ferrari and respected Belgian motoring writer, Paul Frère, tested Alex von Falkenhausen's personal 2002 turbo for *Road & Track* in 1974, and delivered his customary, frank views about the car.

Frère considered the turbo's performance to be beyond risking on normal public roads, and took to BMW's test track to properly explore its outer limits. This particular car was fitted with the optional 6in wide alloy wheels in place of the standard 5.5J steel rims, and Alpina steering wheel, but was without the production car's front chin and boot spoiler. Frère considered the latter to be ugly anyhow. Ugly it might have been, but both proved to be necessary for directional stability at high speed.

Tractable but 'gutless' at low speeds, Frère wrote of the car's 'Jekyll-and-Hyde character', and naturally compared it to the powerful, but normally aspirated, Alpina 2002.

He commented:

Undoubtedly the most impressive thing about the car is its smooth top-end acceleration and the complete lack of fuss with which high cruising speeds can be maintained. Compared with the 165bhp 2002 Alpina I used to own, top-end performance is very similar but very much smoother and more silent (in the Alpina intake roar was the main offender). Thus high-speed cruising – around 110–115mph – is much more relaxed than it was in that highly tuned, unblown car which had practically the same maximum speed. The turbo car uses a higher-geared rear axle (3.36 instead of 3.64:1) and a slight period in the Alpina between 6,000 and 6,200rpm is gone in the turbocharged engine.

Apart from the higher gearing these cars felt fairly dull at low speeds, but also because of the time it took for the blower to reach its full pressure after shoving the throttle pedal to the floor. Turbo lag could take up to 2sec, but Frère found the boost to be progressive, which will come as something of a surprise to the many who considered the shove in the back when the turbo finally cut in to have been dangerous.

Paul Frère's maximum speeds in the gears were recorded as 36mph in First, 65mph in Second, 95mph in Third and 124mph in Fourth, somewhat short of BMW's claimed top speed of 131mph.

TURBO RIVALS

The Alfa Romeo GTV 2000 tested by John Bolster for *Autosport* recorded 30mph in first gear, 51mph in second, 77mph in third and 104mph in fourth. The BMW's best 0–60mph dash recorded by Paul Frère was 8secs, whereas Bolster recorded 9.2secs for

The 1802 with 90bhp joined the range in 1971, but was never as popular with sporting drivers as the 2-litre car.

By 1975 the 2002 story was all but over. As this late car portrays, the styling remained virtually unchanged throughout production. Note that the alloy wheels fitted to this example are 'after-market' items.

the Alfa. The performance benefits of a turbocharger, therefore, were plain enough to appreciate.

This simple 'bolt-on' device gave enormous power potential. The Alfa was one of the quickest and most desirable 2-litre cars of its day, yet the BMW turbo was capable of knocking spots off it. Colin Chapman's beautiful Lotus Elan +2S is also worthy of comparison here. With its lightweight all-fibreglass body and 1600cc twin-cam engine, this little sports car was endowed with impeccable road manners and handling qualities that have rarely been equalled. It was a real flier.

John Bolster tested one for *Autosport* in 1972 and recorded quite outstanding performance figures as follows: First 38mph, Second 62mph, Third 89mph and 120mph in both Fourth and Fifth gears. From 0–60mph the car weighed in at just 7.3secs. The Elan was an exciting motor car, and perceived to be quick because it was a race-derived Lotus. By comparison many viewed the BMW as a rather ordinary looking three-box saloon, but here in the 1970s, was a steel-bodied four-seater capable of keeping pace with a Lotus. It was quite a staggering achievement.

Turbo Dynamics

With respect to handling and roadholding Paul Frère was particularly impressed with the BMW turbo's ability to remain safe and controllable at ludicrously high speeds. It has to be remembered that for a car to impress a man of Frère's lofty motoring stature, it had to be better than exceptional.

He commented:

In the fast curves at the end of the parallel straights of the track, the car felt beautifully stable and neutral with a slight tendency to tuck into the bend if the power was reduced when cornering fast and enough power to powerslide it out of the bend in third when cornering near the limit. But the characteristic 2002 tremor around 50–60mph is still with us, enhanced by the larger steering offset resulting from the use of ventilated front disc brakes and wider

Although this example looks well enough, the 2002 is not a car that lends itself especially well to personalized customizing. The car was just about bang on 'out of the box'.

wheels. Brake fade was never a problem with the Alpina of mine, so it should not be with the turbo either.

In keeping with the rest of the saloon range the rear tail-lamps on the turbo were changed from the classic circular items to less attractive rectangles. The latter were more modern, larger and more easily seen by following motorists, but did little for the car's looks.

With its wheelarch extensions and front and rear spoilers, this was a race car for the road, a real enthusiast's machine but, through no fault of BMW's, it appeared at the wrong time. In the United States it retailed at $6,600 – far from cheap – but there was no shortage of BMW fans for whom the high purchase price was not to prove a deterrent.

The car's real problem was that its launch coincided with the Middle East oil crisis that led to fuel rationing in so many European countries. This killed the BMW 2002 turbo off very quickly, and it was left to the Swedish manufacturer, Saab, to pick up the turbocharged cudgels some years later, after the fuel storm had died down.

A fast, powerful, thirsty motor car in times of fuel rationing was seen as being politically incorrect – Germany's Green movement was beginning to gather momentum – and after the production of just 1,672 examples, production of the glorious 2002 turbo came to an abrupt end. The car became instantly 'collectable' – one of the rarest performance BMWs – and this remains the case today.

... THE WAY THAT YOU DO IT

In Britain, particularly during the 1970s, many patriotic motorists continued to buy British cars. Many genuinely considered BMWs to be no better than the products of Ford and BMC, but merely more expensive. A large part of the purchase price, they argued, was in the acquisition of a name. Some still hold the same view today, but it is one that is unfounded.

Then, as now, the motor industry's potential customers bought motoring magazines containing test reports written by journalists, who expressed their very personal views. The performance figures, however, were carefully recorded and largely accurate by the 1970s. Readers took notice of such figures and bought a car based on its performance, economy or other criteria. But road tests rarely told the entire story.

High top speeds and riveting 0–60mph times make for good bar-bragging fodder, but travelling at 125mph is all well and good, provided that the windscreen wipers aren't trying to tear themselves away from their mountings at such lofty velocity.

As the late John Bolster once commented in *Autosport*:

> Paradoxically, although I spend countless hours taking performance figures, I would advise readers not to pay too much attention to them – it's not what the car does but the way in which it does it that counts.

BMW's cars were certainly more expensive than 'comparable' products in the 2-litre class, but they were also markedly different from the run-of-the-mill. John Bolster added:

> If you want to make a long business journey at high speed, the suspension is much more important than the engine, for if you and your passengers are exhausted by the rough ride, you will not be able to work efficiently when you arrive. Noise is fatiguing, too, and so is excessive roll on corners. Perhaps the

worst vice a car can have is instability in side winds and it's no good having a very fast car if you can't use its maximum when the wind blows; there are also cars that go crazy when it rains and the tester must find out about that also.

BMW were involved in making quality cars that had as few of these defects as possible. In 1972 a 2002 Tii cost £2,299 in Britain. By comparison the 2-litre Vauxhall Firenza was £1,299, the Lotus Europa sporting two-seater was £2,079 and an Opel Rekord Coupé totalled £1,756. The BMW was, therefore, a relatively expensive car in such company, and was even more costly to buy (by £90) than the luxuriously appointed Rover 3500S V8.

With a theoretical top speed of 123mph, the Rover was faster, and such figures when printed in motoring magazines appeared to be important to readers. The importance of largely academic road test data, however, was almost completely forgotten once installed behind the wheel of a BMW. The solidity of German engineering was no more apparent than in the Bavarian cars.

OTHERS CATCH UP

During the mid-1970s a number of respected commentators were seriously beginning to question BMW's justification for charging such high prices for saloon cars. The '02 series had hardly changed since its inception, but their questions were easily answered, despite the looming threat of inexpensive cars from Japanese manufacturers.

Mazda in particular were making headway in the performance stakes with their RX-2 model. But, in the 1600cc–2000cc class, BMW still appeared to command an edge over the competition. In areas of

braking, performance, handling, panel fit and interior comforts, there were few others that scored high marks in all these important parts. Journalists – some begrudgingly – admitted as much.

Technical excellence comes at a price – and usually a heavy one. In a three-way contest between the BMW 2002, Mazda RX-7 and Alfa Romeo 1750 Berlina, *Road & Track* concluded:

> Of course the BMW is better, by a wide margin – but with similar equipment it's over $1400 more expensive and it isn't that much better. The Mazda doesn't come close to being the road machine either the BMW or Alfa is. On this point it's a clear sacrifice. The owner can add a rear anti-roll bar and change to wider wheels and tires and we recommend so doing, but it still won't be a match for the other two.

The reasons, then, for BMWs costing more were apparent. It was the best machine and it wasn't only BMW that thought so.

NEW HEAD GEAR

Towards the end of the 1960s engineers had gone a long way towards answering calls by world legislatures to reduce exhaust emissions. California was once perpetually covered in smog and, rightly or wrongly, the motor car was blamed. The world had to fit in with California, the most lucrative export market. When after 1972 cars brought into the 'Sunshine State' were fitted with low-compression pistons, and ran on unleaded fuel, engine performance suffered significantly.

Several manufacturers, most notably Daimler-Benz, got around the problem of reduced horsepower by installing much larger capacity engines in their passenger cars. Americans who bought American cars moaned and groaned that their steeds felt strangled, while European cars seemed to go properly by comparison.

In the mid-range passenger cars BMW chose to stick with the same capacity engines, which suffered the ignominy of being fitted with the much dreaded air pump. This piece of emissions equipment pushed air drawn from outside into the four exhaust ports, so that carbon monoxide and hydrocarbons would be burnt more efficiently and give cleaner combustion as a result. In conjunction with a lower compression ratio – reduced from 8.5:1 to 8.3:1 for 1972 – the 2002 not only suffered from a drop in power but also had a tendency to backfire on the overrun.

BMW's engineers came up with a clever solution to these problems and did away with the air pump altogether. The 6-cylinder engine introduced in 1968 in the 2800CS (of which more anon) had unique combustion chambers, designed in such a way that the fuel/air mixture burned sufficiently cleanly to meet emissions legislation thus obviating the need for an air pump.

Curved 'domes' on top of the pistons, spherical chambers in which the sparking plugs were located and semi-spherical chambers for the valves, created something akin to a relief map of the floor of volcanic parts of the Pacific Ocean. Nevertheless, it worked and gave acceptable emissions in conjunction with unimpaired performance. This design was, therefore, copied and transferred to the 4-cylinder cars.

BMW had a name for the design, too – the *Dreikugelwirbelwannenbrenraum* (tri-spherical turbulence-inducing combustion chamber) – that not surprisingly didn't form the centrepiece of conversation among BMW enthusiasts in non-German-speaking countries.

The 1.6-litre car was reintroduced to the range in 1974 as a fuel-thrifty 'entry-level' BMW. Its specification differed from market to market, and the car finally bowed out in 1977 a year after the introduction of the 3 series.

The result was a 2002 that had reverted to its original performance of the mid-1960s, that in terms of progress had stood still in eight years of production. Some described the car as being well beyond its 'sell-by' date, yet there was still little to equal it in its class. 'If everyone drove one of these cars,' remarked *Road & Track*, 'traffic would move a lot more quickly.'

Few could find real fault with the 2002, but BMW recognized that the range was getting long in the tooth, and was busy developing the 3 Series which arrived in 1976 as a replacement.

CRISIS AT 16

The 1973 oil crisis in the Middle East had far-reaching consequences for motor manufacturers and their customers. The whole charade had seen fuel rationing, and this had not only killed off 'supercars' like the 2002 turbo, but really forced car makers to think seriously about producing far more fuel-efficient engines.

This imposed goal would take many years to achieve, and not even BMW's talented people could work a miracle overnight. The engineers could give no immediate help in improving fuel efficiency, which is why the marketing men were forced to pull out all the stops to ensure that BMWs continued to sell well, and promptly, despite the world-wide economic crisis. BMW weren't alone in relying on clever marketing.

In Wolfsburg Volkswagen reintroduced a crudely appointed version of the Beetle. It was largely devoid of external and internal trim, had a headlining that wasn't extended to the roof pillars and was without 'full size' hubcaps. These were penny pinching measures designed to save money for Volkswagen and for customers at the showroom. BMW's equivalent strategy was the

reintroduction of the 1602 in 1974, that had been dropped from the range just two years earlier.

Bright body colours, including a totally unforgettable shade of green, wider 5J wheels with exposed hub nuts and devoid of hubcaps, and a revised radiator grille in matt black were all part of the 1602 package. But essentially the car hadn't changed in nearly a decade.

PRESENT IN THE PAST

The diminutive 1,573cc single overhead-camshaft engine developed 85bhp which, employed in the chassis designed to accept the more powerful 2-litre unit, allowed enthusiastic drivers to exploit their skills to the full without coming to too much grief. More important for many, though, this was an inexpensive BMW. In Britain this 'entry-level' car retailed at a very reasonable £1,999, a whisker under the 'watershed' £2,000 barrier. The 1602 Special was also available at the slightly higher price of £2,249.

The latter version had front and rear anti-roll bars, rubber bumper overriders, a heated rear window, tachometer in place of a clock and a brace of foglamps. There was even a Luxus version with more comfortable seats and superfluous trim which, ironically, was available on the entry-level car at extra cost. Although the 1602 was considered to be, and marketed as, a 'budget' BMW, it was still twice as expensive to buy as a VW Beetle, for example. However, by this time, BMW had gone to great lengths to cultivate its sporting image and sales remained healthy.

The 1974 1602 benefited from a very slight gain in pulling power over the original pre-1972 model. This was achieved by replacing the Solex 38 PDSI carburettor

The 3 series superseded the '02 range in 1976, and although acknowledged as a superior and more modern design, purists bemoaned a slight loss of character.

with a Solex 40 PDSI unit, and there was an increase in torque from 91lb/ft at 3,000rpm to 95.4lb/ft of torque at 3,500rpm. Despite optimistic speedometer readings on the majority of production cars, the 1602 was capable of a good honest 100mph. By comparison, the 1600cc VW Beetle that produced 50bhp was good for a top speed of 80mph.

Geared for 16.3mph per 1,000rpm in fourth, the BMW's engine revolved at 5,500rpm at 90mph, yet mechanical noise inside the cabin was never obtrusive, and was always at lower levels than its less expensive rivals in this class.

Stuart Bladon tested a 1602 in France for *Autocar* in May 1974 and, like so many other journalists, found it very much to his liking. He was particularly enamoured with its handling, levels of grip generated by the Michelin 165×13 radial tyres and high-

speed stability in crosswinds. On the other hand Bladon, like so many of his contemporaries, considered the design to be 'old hat'.

He commented:

In some respects one is reminded that the body of the 1602 is now somewhat dated, particularly in such matters as lack of face-level ventilation or rear extraction. In fact, it is necessary to open the rear side windows to get reasonable air-flow through the car, and the heater has only a water-valve control.

This was niggling, nit-picking criticism – true nonetheless – but criticism just the same. On the other hand Bladon went on:

But the good ride, positive steering and predictable and very manageable behaviour in fast cornering, allied to the performance offered make it still very competitive.

The English magazine *Motor* tested the special version in July 1974 and came down on it for its high purchase price, poor ventilation and spartan fittings. This journal's testers, however, liked its excellent road manners, nice gear change, build quality and willing engine – all the things for which BMW had become respected the world over.

In terms of handling and performance the Triumph Dolomite Sprint, with its 16-valve cylinder head and advanced chassis, would easily outperform the BMW. And it was cheaper to buy. Set against the 'Dolly' Sprint, however, was an appalling reliability record, indifferent build quality and the usual heap of problems that came at no extra cost from British Leyland in the 1970s.

The *Motor* rated the Ford Escort RS 2000, Lancia Beta, Opel Manta, Mazda RX-4 and Vauxhall Magnum 2300 as the BMW's most competent rivals. It's interesting, though, that a 2.3-litre Vauxhall was considered to be equal to a 1.6-litre BMW. Other manufacturers had, at long last, caught up with BMW – few had overtaken them.

A FINAL FLING

Minor production modifications to the '02 range for 1974 included a redesigned instrument panel and steering wheel – a four-spoker with a large central pad and horn buttons in all four spokes – revised seats with integral head restraints, revised rear lamps, and wider front and rear track, but this was a car reaching the end of its development.

With a respectable 0–60mph time of 11.9secs the 1602 was as quick as most of its rivals, but average fuel mileage worked out little better than 21mpg, at a time when a 3-litre Ford Capri could return nearly 20mpg. Journalists complained but few owners did. A *Road & Track* survey showed that 89 per cent of owners were happy with their cars, and content to buy another BMW.

Motor's journalists came down on the car for excessive clutch pedal travel, heavy steering at parking speeds, lack of progressive braking response, cramped rear passenger compartment and whine from the cooling fan, but admitted that it was still a driver's car in the best tradition.

From one point of view, American and British journalists clearly didn't understand German automotive thinking, and revealed their lack of insight on many occasions. Dashboard instrumentation, for example, which comprised an oil pressure and fuel gauge on the left, speedometer in the centre and tachometer on the right, gave all the information about the car's mechanical health at a glance in a small, confined space.

To many the 2002 has never been replaced; it is the car that brought BMW into the modern era, and gave the company the high reputation it enjoys for producing quality sporting saloons today.

As is well known this was for safety's sake – to prevent the driver looking away from the road – but journalists interpreted this design philosophy as being in pursuit of austerity. Daimler-Benz and Volkswagen have operated the same policy for decades, whereas Jaguar, Aston-Martin and others of similar persuasion have done precisely the opposite. Emulating the interior of a jet aeroplane doubtless gives an impression of high-tech efficiency, but rows of gauges for separate functions are not only unnecessary and expensive, but provide a first-class opportunity for distracting the driver.

CONCLUSION

By the mid-1970s the German economy was in a healthy state of tune and, despite the high value of the mark, car exports were similarly healthy and increasing. Germany's manfacturing base was booming and there was good reason for optimism at BMW. The 2002 was still a competitive motor car in its final year of production, despite the oft-quoted bleating in the international press, but BMW knew the dangers of resting on past laurels all too well and replaced the '02 range with the 3 Series.

Whether 1602, 1802 or 2002, these cars were highly regarded for what they were – beautifully engineered, well-built sporting four-seaters for those who wanted something different from their motoring. Used cars continued to sell well long after production had been halted in 1976 and commanded high prices.

In this series BMW had created a true classic which, with the benefit of hindsight, hadn't really got a true rival. These cars were always stimulating to drive, and had

At a modern BMW club meeting today, the '02s are as much in evidence as the early 3-series cars.

all the styling attributes of the crispness of the Bavarian character.

POSTSCRIPT

Although production of the 1602, 1802 and 2002 bowed out in stages between 1975 and 1976, the 1502 was reintroduced in 1975. This was a basic 1600 which continued in production until 1977. The engine had reverted to a single Solex 38 PDSI carburettor and developed 75bhp at 5,800rpm with a 8:1 compression ratio.

It came with plain steel wheels and chromed hubcaps, and was intended as an inexpensive entry-level car for impecunious younger people. In its two-year production run, 72,632 units were made and sold, retailing in Germany at DM11,390, well below the cost of the 'first rung' 3 series.

All things considered it was this New Class '02 range that had not only saved BMW from an uncertain future, but had also paved the way for the creation of almost unimaginable prosperity. By 1976 BMWs were considered to be *the* top sporting saloons. Success on the race track – big success – had helped. The company had its own testing facilities, a massive office complex, the factory was churning out between 800 and 1,000 cars per day and these figures would quickly rise.

Autocar summed up both the German automotive industry and BMW during 1972. The magazine commented in a general editorial about this success as follows:

Germany at the moment is suffering from chronic efficiency. No part of the Federation has this disease more than Munich, and in this case there seems to be two main causes. The pending Olympics have given the city a sense of purpose and a multi-million pound facelift, and the recent rise to fame of the Bayerische Motor Werke has produced an almost clinically efficient industrial complex.

The symbol of this new found wealth at BMW is an 18 storey office block which dominates Munich's factory skyline and casts a shadow across the nearly completed Olympic village which stands at its feet.

Another and immediately more beneficial development by BMW is the construction of a proving ground on the outskirts of the city. Covering more than 600 acres and with 13 miles of roads the circuit is equipped to simulate almost any combination of road and weather conditions.

A similar test facility was owned and run by Porsche near Stuttgart and, like BMW's, was paid for from profits. This facet of the German motor industry is important. It has ensured its continued success.

5 The Big BMWs: Guns Aimed at Stuttgart

SIX CYLINDERS

THE GRAND TOUR

In centuries long since past it was the domain of rich aristocrats to undertake a journey on horseback, or in a horse-drawn carriage, around Continental Europe. Such inherently uncomfortable sojourns were undertaken over rough, unmade roads to the great cities – Paris, Rome, Vienna and others – and lasted several weeks or months.

The purpose of these trips, that became known as the Grand Tour, was cultural exchange, education, a broadening-of-the-mind, enriching-of-the-soul exercise and a means of spreading political and economic influence among like-minded folks in non-English-speaking countries.

In terms of the sheer physical energy required to undertake such a journey, the modern equivalent might be competing on the annual Paris–Dakar raid on a single-cylinder 50cc moped, or perhaps taking a trans-Atlantic flight in the baggage hold of a Boeing 747 but, for the privileged few during the centuries leading up to the one in which the motor car was invented, the Grand Tour was an essential part of a civilized person's agenda.

Such journeys continued to be undertaken by the rich into the 1930s, and the only aspect of this Grand Tour that had changed was the time it took to reach the various capital cities. Motor manufacturers in

With its restyled front end and twin headlamps, the 2800CS Coupé replaced the 2000C and CS models in 1968–69. The all-new 2.8-litre 6-cylinder engine was clearly aimed at both Porsche and Daimler-Benz.

A handsome motor car by any standards, the big coupés were also fast and luxuriously appointed. The bodies were once again built by Karmann to the highest standards, even though rust would become this model's principal enemy in the years ahead.

Pillarless doors continued as a most elegant styling concept on these coupés.

France, Italy, Germany and Britain recognized the importance of providing wealthy folks with increasingly opulent vehicles in which Continental Touring could be undertaken.

It is strongly argued that the greatest of these GT cars was the Bentley Continental R, of which there were just 207 examples built between 1952 and 1955. With stylish two-door coupé bodywork by H.J. Mulliner, a magnificent 4.6-litre (or 4.9-litre) 6-cylinder engine, and the ability to cruise at over 100mph in almost silent comfort, these were Grand Tourers in the finest tradition.

However, by the 1950s, their owners rarely undertook the kind of mileages on

The beautiful pre-War 328 model boasted an advanced specification and a fabulous 6-cylinder engine, facets of Munich engineering that have never changed.

The famous blue and white aeroplane 'propeller' badge and 'kidney' radiator grille have been BMW hallmarks since the 1930s.

A combination of evocative styling and practical considerations are typical of BMW's way of doing things.

(Above) No modern vintage meeting would be complete without a 328 taking part.

(Below) The 'Baroque Angels' of the 1950s were expensive and luxurious, but there were few customers. By 1959 BMW's future was seriously in doubt.

Built by Karmann, the 4-cylinder 2000CS's frontal styling was controversial, but provided a sound basis for the classic 6-cylinder coupés.

The 1500–2000 range of cars revived BMW's fortunes in the 1960s, the larger-engined versions particularly appealing to sporting drivers.

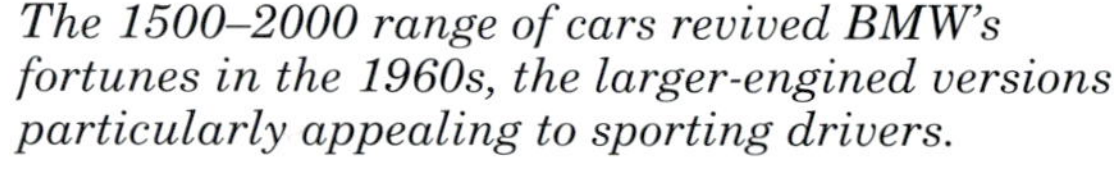

With the launch of the '02 series in the mid-1960s, BMW never looked back.

Many motoring aficionados often cited the 2002 as the finest sports saloon of the 1960s and '70s.

(Above) Cabriolet versions of the 2002 were built in relatively small numbers, and provided fans of fresh air with exhilarating motoring.

(Below) Arguably the world's first 'hot-hatch', the three-door Touring version was added to the range in 1971, and provided fast, safe, family transport.

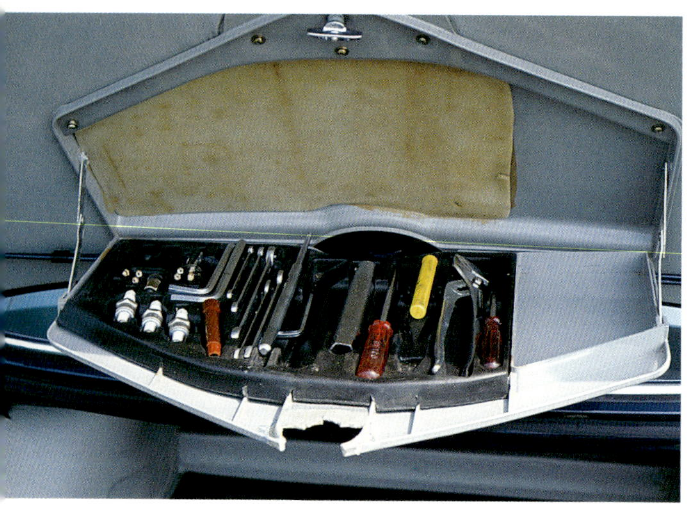

(Above Left) A comprehensive toolkit attached to the underside of the rear lid is one of many innovative details that project BMW head and shoulders above the 'herd'.

(Above Right) BMW's modern in-line 6-cylinder engines began in 1968 with the 2.8-litre; in terms of performance and refinement the 'sixes' are widely regarded as the benchmark standard by which all other power units are measured.

(Right) The CS Coupé's steering wheel is overly large, the wood veneer curiously incongruous and there's an automatic gearbox largely for the benefit of the lucrative American market, but there's no doubting BMW's 'no nonsense' approach to ergonomics in the late 1960s and early 1970s.

(Below) The Karmann-built CS Coupés were arguably the best-looking cars of their generation – true classics in every sense – which BMW have never improved on.

(Above) The 3-litre version of the CS is an all-time classic that makes for perfectly practical transport in modern times.

(Below) Lightweight CSL coupés are among the most coveted of all BMWs, although values have not kept pace with those of contemporary Italian exotica.

(Above) The sensational 'Batmobile' was a limited edition, homologation 'special' that gave Ford of Cologne something to think hard about during the early 1970s.

(Left) Elegant, spacious, quick and comfortable, the 6-cylinder 2500/2800/3.0 saloons arrived in the late 1960s as a real alternative to 'barge-like' Mercs.

(Below) The stunning M1 thrilled crowds in the 'one-make' series for these cars in the 1980s.

(Above) Works driver Dieter Quester remained successful in BMW racing cars for more than three decades.

(Below) Launched in 1972 the 5 series established the Munich company as the maker of some of the world's finest automobiles.

(Below) Typically Germanic in every sense, the 5 series cut a trend of engineering excellence that continues to this day.

Many argue that the post-1982 5 series was the last of the classic BMW sporting saloons.

A symbol of excellence and fine engineering integrity throughout the world.

one trip that their ancestors had endured. Bentley Continentals were at their best conveying their lucky owners from the home counties of England to the gambling casinos of Monte-Carlo on the French Riviera. Such activity was hardly the cultural and educational exchange it had once been but, by the 1950s, Britain and Europe were much changed places.

By the mid-1960s there wasn't a car made anywhere that wasn't capable of being driven from northern climes to the south of France, which is why a plethora of mundane saloons were badged as GTs. These included cars like Ford's 1500cc Cortina. These weren't Grand Tourers in the true or tradi-tional sense. All that the GT badges did was to distinguish them from their slightly less powerful sisters in the range.

Grand Tourers continued to be built; they included cars from Bristol, Bentley and Daimler-Benz, and Ferrari-produced sporting versions, of course, but there was a huge gap in the market created by the emergence of the affluent middle classes. This occurred in the 1960s and no-one capitalized on it better than BMW. During the 1950s the company had built luxury cars, but they were 'gutless', had quite unacceptable styling and customers were few and far between. BMW weren't going to get their fingers burnt by repeating mistakes of the past.

In the manner of traditional British designs, wood veneer was used for the dashboard, door cappings and gear lever knob. The deeply dished steering wheel was, in contemporary German fashion, far too large.

Conveniently and neatly positioned, the toolkit sits under the rear lid.

Although designed as a full four-seater, legroom in the rear is restricted in the manner of most luxury tourers.

Upholstery was in high-quality cloth, or leather (as here) at extra cost.

The wide, heavy doors originally had manually operated windows, with the rear windows driven by electric motors controlled by the driver.

THE NEED TO TRAVEL

By 1968 when BMW launched the first of the 'big sixes', Germany had an extensive Autobahn network, and people were using them to travel vast distances on a daily basis at high speeds. Business executives regularly notched up huge annual mileages, and there wasn't one car up until 1968 that catered perfectly for their needs.

The 'under 40s' saw Mercedes saloons as cars for older folks – the image was wrong – and the SL two-seater sports cars were incapable of carrying a family of four. The same applied to the Porsche 911. What the 'upwardly mobile' required was a fast, comfortable, sports tourer that didn't cost an arm and a leg to buy and run, and was, at the same time, practical.

In some respects a Mercedes-Benz saloon fitted the bill, except that Mercs were stolid, heavy, flabby and generally not very pretty. A new type of car was required. BMW were looking to expand into 'luxus' territory and, as in the past, turned their attention to a new 6-cylinder car.

OLD PROVIDES FOR NEW

In 1966 BMW's engineers took the tried and trusty 4-cylinder engine as the basis for the 6-cylinder unit, and redesigned the cylinder head – the *Dreikugelwirbelwannen-brenraum* described in a previous chapter. A big six was an obvious choice to propel a sporting saloon of such exquisite proportions as the 2800CS launched in 1968. There is a strong case for arguing that BMW have not made a better-looking car, before or since, than this magnificent 'flagship' coupé.

The CS was built on foundations already laid down by the Karmann built 2000CS, but the less satisfactory parts of the 2-litre car were redesigned with spectacularly good results. The proportions and dimensions of the 2000CS's all-steel monocoque hull were retained, and steel was used for the two doors and front and rear lids, but the styling detail gave the car a lean, hungry, purposeful and aggressive look.

At the front the famous kidney grille was retained, naturally, but the grilles to the left and right were in matt black and contained twin circular headlamps – a long-lasting BMW feature. The 2000CS's height and width was considered about right for a car of this nature, but the 6-cylinder car's nose was extended by 3in, which inevitably required new front wings and a longer bonnet.

The BMW roundel on the rear roof pillar cleverly doubles as an air outlet for the cabin ventilation system.

The rectangular front indicators were incorporated into the side of the front wings and, unlike the integrated wrap-around items fitted to the 2-litre cars, were wholly separate from the headlamps. Both the front and rear bumpers, that had integral overriders and rubber inserts, were elegant, slimmer and gave the car a less heavy appearance. Horizontal louvres for extracting hot engine air were built into the front wings behind the wheel arches, and added to the car's sporting appearance as well as being practical.

All four wheel arches were flared to accommodate larger wheels and tyres, and the aesthetic result was the same – a more purposeful and sporting appearance. Bright mouldings ran along the flanks and sill, or rocker, panels, the latter of which gave an illusion of a much lower car than the one from which it was developed. Neat, unique features, such as the BMW roundels on the 'C' pillars doubled as cabin ventilation outlets, as they had on the 2000CS. As before the doors were also pillarless.

One other huge improvement in looks was provided by the 6Jx14 cast-alloy wheels. These were to an attractive five-spoke design with the same number of rectangular vents between the spokes. These were much more in keeping with trends of the late 1960s than the plain steel items and chromed hubcaps that had seen service on the 2-litre cars. Happily, Michelin XAS 175 HR14 radial tyres were employed as standard rubberware.

Looking in

Inside the cabin, which had been thoughtfully redesigned, there were few of the fussy features to be found in Italian machinery, nor the opulence, for example, of an Aston-Martin. The interior was in typical German fashion, the result of a quest to find a formula of function over form. There were touches of luxury and hectares of comfort – a tasteful piece of restrained class – although the veneer parts of the dashboard and door cappings were incongruous in this archetypal German machine.

A full four-seater of generous proportions, the front and rear seats were beautifully shaped to take account of both long-journey comfort and lateral support during hard cornering. Deeply fluted and generously padded, vinyl or cloth was provided as standard although leather – rare in Britain – was available at extra cost.

Breathing through a brace of Solex 35/40 INAT carburettors the 2.8-litre engine produces a maximum of 192bhp at 6,000rpm, and close to 130mph performance at the 'top end'.

Both front seats had adjustable head restraints, and the fully reclining backrests were adjustable with levers on their outsides. The hinges between the squabs and backrests were to the same bold design as those in the 2000CS. These were not only functional (and given to breaking in old age), but added a touch of luxury in an age when bright trim was gradually becoming less important at both ends of the car market.

One particularly thoughtful piece of design was the location of the toolkit, which was placed on the underside of the rear lid. For years manufacturers had traditionally supplied tools in a plastic roll-up bag, often placed in a deeply inaccessible part of the luggage compartment. Over a period of time this bag would crack, become encrusted in oil and grime, and even a simple job like changing a wheel on the side of the road would become a necessarily mucky and horrible task.

BMW solved this by making a neat plastic box, the base of which could be unscrewed by hand, and folded down to reveal a pristine and comprehensive set of tools. This was one of many features that set aside BMWs from the herd, and the company is to be applauded for continuing with this toolkit arrangement to this day. The floor of the boot was fully carpeted and concealed the horizontally positioned spare wheel below in a purpose shaped well.

The outwardly similar 3.0CS arrived in 1970–71, the larger engine bringing the benefit of increased torque and performance.

Information without Technology

The layout of the instruments and controls was in BMW's characteristic workmanlike manner. There was none of the ornateness of so many Grand Touring machines. Four deeply set and shrouded instruments confronted the driver. Left to right they consisted of a combination fuel/water temperature gauge, speedometer, tachometer and 'obligatory' clock. All were circular, simply styled with black backgrounds, white characters and chromium-plated bezels. The binnacle had a wood veneer surround.

Heating and ventilation controls, cigar lighter, radio and switches to operate the electric windows were positioned on the central console. The windscreen wipers and indicators were operated by stalks mounted on the right and left of the steering column, the left one also doubling as a headlamp flasher. The headlamp switch itself was to the left of the steering column. Right-hand drive cars had these arrangements reversed.

This was all very neatly packaged and the dashboard was 'stepped', so that the flat surface between the instrument binnacle and glovebox on the passenger's side could be used for storing odds and ends. Again the steering wheel was, in Daimler-Benz fashion, absurdly large, but at least made for easy operation in low-speed driving or parking.

A three-spoker, the steering wheel was deeply dished for safety, and had a black padded horn button in the centre devoid of decoration. BMW might have considered placing a company motif here, but they didn't, and customers were surprised. As *Road & Track*'s February 1970 road test pointed out:

There is no BMW identification anywhere in the interior – you don't need to be reminded of what car you are driving. But the BMW badge appears eight times on the exterior – others are being informed!

Leather was used to trim the rim of the wheel, and the gear knob was in either leather or wood according to different markets. The floor-mounted gear lever sat in the centre between the front seats with the handbrake lever directly behind it.

In both left- and right-hand drive guises, these cars were ergonomically well conceived. Even the pedals on right-hand drive cars were well spaced, which certainly hadn't always been the case with cars converted for the benefit of the British and Japanese. All controls were within easy reach and felt solidly made.

With such a deep dashboard and steeply curved windscreen, the driver and passenger sat well back – away from the dashboard – which helped to promote a feeling of safety, or remoteness from danger, even if this was only illusory.

Heart of the Matter

For the powerplant, BMW took its usual route of cast-iron for the 6-cylinder, in-line block, and aluminium-alloy for the single-overhead camshaft cylinder head, both pieces representing engneering sculpture at their best. With a bore and stroke of 86×80mm, overall capacity worked out at 2,788cc (170cu in). A modest compression ratio of 9:1 was considered adequate and, with a brace of Solex 35/40 INAT carburettors, maximum power of 192bhp was developed at 6,000rpm. Maximum torque of 194lb ft was developed at 3,780rpm. In true tradition the unit was positioned well forward in the chassis to give predominately understeering handling characteristics.

Of this unit *Car & Driver* remarked: 'Its engine is grossly extravagant by Detroit

BMW rivals included the ever-present Porsche 911, a serious sports car in every sense, but with limited appeal for those with a need to carry more than one passenger.

standards – you certainly don't need a powerplant built like a Rolex – but that is the appeal of a BMW.'

Cooling was by entirely conventional means, with a large radiator up front and jackets around the cylinder block – nothing fancy or complex, but just plain common-sense engineering. It is typical of BMW that the engine compartment was as nicely made and finished as the exterior of the car, and gave a large hint as to the purpose and dynamics of the engine itself.

No-one who has ever driven one of these cars failed to be impressed by the engine, for it was truly remarkable and has rarely been surpassed, except perhaps by BMW's modern 'sixes' and 'twelves'. *Road & Track*'s testers were untypically restrained in their description of the car's performance and commented:

Driving moderately, the 2800CS is smooth and very, very quiet. At cruising speeds the only sound is the steady hum of the steel-belted Michelin XAS tires. The big BMW engine is without a doubt, the most efficient and sophisticated in-line six in the world. It is powerful and responsive, yet remarkably easy on gasoline and meets government emission regulations on carburettors with no added-on devices. Almost soundlessly willing at part-throttle, with amazingly low tappet noise, it has the most beautifully subdued snarl imaginable when opened up. Getting off in a hurry is accompanied by traditional BMW wheel patter – not objectionable but one of the few things about the car that is not ultra-refined.

A top speed of 127mph was achievable with consummate ease. Floor the throttle at almost any speed, and the car simply eased forward with the grace and 'grunt' of a healthy adult killer whale in search of a large meal. With a curb weight of 2,990lb, this was no lightweight but despite this, the car was well capable of achieving 60mph from standstill in 9.3secs. With an 18.5-gallon fuel tank in the tail, it also had a good cruising range of 370 miles and reasonable average fuel mileage of around 20mpg.

BMW 2800CS (1968–70)

Layout and Chassis	Unitary construction, two-door coupé

Engine

Type	In-line
Block material	Cast-iron with conventional water jackets
Cylinder head	Light alloy
Cylinders	Six
Cooling	Water
Bore × stroke	86 × 80mm
Capacity	2,788cc (170cu in)
Valves	Two per cylinder
Timing	Single ohc
Compression ratio	9:1
Maximum power	192bhp at 6,000rpm
Maximum torque	194 lb ft at 3,780rpm
Fuel system	Two Solex 35/40 INAT carburettors
Fuel tank capacity	14.6gal (66ltr)

Transmission

Gearbox	Synchromesh 4-speed manual
Ratios	First 3.85
	Second 2.08
	Third 1.38
	Fourth 1.00
	Final drive 3.45
Clutch	Single dry-plate

Suspension and steering

Front	Independent by MacPherson struts, coil springs and anti-roll bar
Rear	Independent by semi trailing arms, coil springs and anti-roll bar
Steering	Power-assisted recirculating ball, with 4 turns lock to lock
Tyres	HR14 radial
Wheels	Cast alloy 14inx6in

Brakes	Hydraulically operated, power-assisted discs (front), drums (rear)

Dimensions (in/mm)

Track	Front 57/1,448
	Rear 55/1,397
Wheelbase	103/2,616
Overall length	184/4661
Overall width	66/1,669
Overall height	54/1,372
Dry weight	3,025lb (1,372kg)

Performance

Maximum speed	127mph (204km/h)
0–60mph (0–100km)	9.3sec
Standing quarter mile (0.4km)	16.4sec
Fuel consumption	15–22mpg (12.9–18.9ltr × 100km)

The 2800CS was superseded in 1971 by the 3.0CS. This model had a bore and stroke of 89 × 80mm, capacity of 2,985cc, compression ratio of 9:1 and dual Zenith carburettors. Top speed rose to 133mph (214km/h). In addititon there were disc brakes front and rear. The fuel-injected 3.0CSi was launched in 1972; for its details, see the main text.

Rivals in the Field

The BMW's performance and all-round ability compared well with arch-rivals from Daimler-Benz, Jaguar and Porsche. The Porsche 911 was a different kind of car, a 2+2 for individualists who needed something radically different from 'mainstream' to express their motoring desires. Jaguar's E-Type (dubbed XKE in North America) had a much higher top speed – a shade under 150mph – but, in terms of build quality and practical considerations, it was in a different league.

The Jaguar XJ6, also launched in 1968, found favour in Britain, but even dyed-in-the-wool Jaguar people occasionally despaired at the car's seemingly unquenchable thirst for breaking back axles and overheating. During the 1970s it was also discovered that the XJ6, and subsequent 12-cylinder cars, had a propensity for rusting badly.

Daimler-Benz's 'Pagoda' roof 280SL sports car boasted similar properties to those of the 2800CS. There was an in-line 6-cylinder engine, superb build quality, fabulous handling, good performance and handsome looks. On the other hand, though, the Stuttgart machine could only comfortably accommodate two adults, and a couple of little 'uns at a push.

The only problem the 2800CS had to fight in such hallowed company was its purchase price. In the United States the BMW cost $8,107, a fraction over the psychologically important eight thousand barrier. Customers raised their eyebrows and naturally compared this price with the Mercedes SL ($7,654), Porsche 911E ($7,995), and almost incomprehensively inexpensive Jaguar XKE which was listed at just $6,250.

BMW's marketing people were clearly pushing their luck – they needed too – and came out smiling. With electrically operated windows, sunroof, air-conditioning, automatic transmission, tinted windows and a radio – all extra-cost options – the overall price nudged to $10,000, and Americans during this period, did not usually buy a 'little' 6-cylinder 120cu in 'cutey' from Europe at such a high price.

Jaguar's E-Type was a fast two-seater with ageless styling and good road manners – it was also inexpensive – but build quality was to Britain's usual standards, and Munich were only too happy to pick up the pieces.

However, as *Road & Track* pointed out:

> The BMW is a far more stable, balanced, totally usable car than any other we can think of, and there is nothing remotely approaching the 2800CS for significantly less. One has to look to the top-of-the-line Mercedes-Benz models, or to the Ferrari/ Lamborghini class, to find more car. So anyone with $9,000 to spend must find the 2800CS close to irresistible.

Capable of 32mph in bottom gear, 61mph in second, 91mph in third, 127mph in fourth and a sub-29sec 0–100mph time, the BMW was a truly modern Grand Tourer in the traditional sense. The torque of the engine was considered to be sufficient to warrant the use of a 4- rather than 5-speed gearbox. This was mounted directly to the engine, with the propshaft inclined at a shallow angle to the differential and final-drive unit at the rear. The gear ratios were as follows: First 3.85:1, Second 2.12:1, Third 1.38:1, Fourth 1:1, Final-drive 3.45:1. This was sensible, usable gear spacing without discernible gaps, and the shift was almost universally praised for its swiftness and smoothness in operation.

Trailing Behind

For the suspension BMW found no good reason to change from the previously tried and tested formula. At the front there were the ubiquitous MacPherson struts, lower wishbones, coil springs, hydraulic shock absorbers and an anti-roll bar. At the rear were semi-trailing arms, coil springs, hydraulic dampers and an anti-roll bar. With weight distribution front to rear of 56/44, the car's handling and roadholding properties were just about unrivalled in the 'big car' class.

Car & Driver were unequivocal in their assessment of the car's roadability. They commented:

> The 2800CS has fully independent suspension – MacPherson struts at the front and semi-trailing arms in the rear – but there is more to it than that. The secret is that, as soon as you get off the autobahns, Germany is bumpy and the guys who tune the BMW suspension would be derelict in their duties if they didn't make the car perform well on their own roads. But never mind the reason. It is the result that you're driving and it works. You might say BMW engineers

A minor work of automotive art, the Ferrari Dino 246 (launched in 1968) cost roughly the same to buy as BMW's big coupé, but . . .

developed a competent suspension system out of necessity, but it is the precision intricacies of engines that they enjoy and you don't have to drive the 2800CS long to affirm the fact.

Although inherently inclined towards understeer, hanging the tail end out by judicious prodding of the throttle pedal was, and remains, one of life's most joyous pastimes, to be indulged in frequently by proponents of the art of 'opposite lock'.

As *Car & Driver* put it:

You'll fare a whole lot better if you confine your competitive urges to twisting back roads where cubic inches don't call the shots. Flailing within the limits of sanity on public roads is a serene occupation and only when you go all out on a road course do you discover that the BMW is basically an understeering car.

To really understand why these cars cost so much to buy, though, it was necessary to live with one for a whole lot longer than the brief period in which test journalists drove them. At any speed up to 100mph the cabin was almost silent. Bang the throttle pedal to the floor, and virtually anything ahead could be overtaken with ease and safety. As an 'inter-state' cruiser it was only rivalled by the big V8 engined Mercs.

But the Mercs lost out as all-rounders. The Stuttgart machines couldn't be hustled along country lanes, as they were too big and ungainly. So was the Jaguar XJ6. The BMW on the other hand felt like a 'grown up' 2002 – nimble, lithe and shark-like, as its frontal appearance suggested.

To put the car more in context, the Shelby Mustang could be had for $4,434 in 1969, or virtually half the cost of the 2800CS, but the difference between the two cars could be compared to that between a bottle of lemonade and one of Champagne. The former is perfectly drinkable and serves its purpose. The latter is also perfectly drinkable, but is also exciting and has a great deal more to offer in every way.

Room for Improvement

In view of the immense power of the engine, it is anomalous that this big Coupé had a conventional braking system with 10.7in diameter discs at the front and 9.8in diameter drums at the rear. Discs would have been a better choice all round. Such as they were the brakes were power-assisted, and the swept braking area totalled a reasonable 394sq in.

By comparison with other German sports cars, *Road & Track* found the braking system to be unsatisfactory. *Car & Driver*'s staff came to the same conclusion, although the writer of their December 1969 report was keen to point out that the BMW's brakes might not have been entirely to blame for such poor anchor performance. He remarked:

The system is beautifully modulated so that lock-up of the fronts and rears occurs at precisely the same instant and the pedal is so sensitive that you can avoid or induce lock-up as you see fit. The latter attribute was particularly important during the braking test because the tires (Phoenix Senators, if that means anything to you) lost a significant portion of their deceleration force when they started to slide. The result is that, even though the thought of a more controllable braking system stretches our imagination, the 288ft (0.74G) required to stop the BMW from 80mph is not a very meritorious achievement and we have put the evil eye on the tires.

As far as technology allowed, tyre companies had just about perfected radials by 1969. Had crossplies continued to predominate, though, it is doubtful that BMW would have even bothered to build the 6-cylinder cars. Knowledgeable customers, who both enjoyed driving and possessed real skill at the wheel, were well aware that Michelin and Pirelli made the best tyres. Anything less was rather second-rate. Complaining about the 2800CS's inability to brake satisfactorily was one thing, but the car's shortcomings on a set of Phoenix Senators is quite another! This was asking a little too

Like its rivals from Stuttgart and Maranello, the 3.0CS had elegant styling and excellent performance, but BMW also had the advantage of good fuel mileage.

much of the BMW, but the people in Munich would take notice of this criticism for the future nonetheless.

For steering the car utilized the power-assisted ZF-Gemmer worm and roller system. This gave a reasonable turning circle between kerbs of 34.5ft, and needed four complete turns of the steering wheel from lock to lock. *Road & Track*'s assessment of the steering probably didn't go down very well in Munich. Writer of the magazine's February 1970 test commented:

> The power steering is nearly as good as that of Mercedes, which is to say, tops. It feels just a bit light initially at high speeds but continued use of the car builds complete confidence; there is just enough feel to ensure accuracy. At lower speeds, the CS is really maneuvrable.

Hooked on a BMW

For many years Daimler-Benz and Porsche have produced the world's best engineered vehicles. Daimler-Benz have no excuse for not doing so; they, after all, invented the motor car. Likewise, Porsche have no excuse; this company has been blessed with a family of genius to guide it through the twentieth century.

BMW, however, were 'born-again' newcomers to the luxury sports car market, and had made a laudable stab at their first attempt. The steering might not have been quite on a par with the big Mercs, but it was pretty damned close, and to be compared with Stuttgart's best first time out of the box, was quite an achievement.

The 2800CS was an aristocratic machine that, in many aspects of its design, particularly the 6-cylinder engine, set new standards. Styling was simply fabulous. Detroit had nothing to equal it at any price. American manufacturers had a different philosophy, certainly, but generally their cars were technologically crude – about which they cared little – and built to a standard that German manufacturers could not conceive. Detroit churned out cheap, cheerful, powerful cars that satisfied a need.

As beautifully built as they undoubtedly were, the S class Mercs were never in the same sporting league as the 6-cylinder BMWs, and felt ungainly to drive by comparison.

Exterior badging was bold and stylish.

But, as *Car & Driver* pointed out:

The entire BMW formula for success is predicated on the fact that you don't need one of their cars – you buy it because you can't resist. Drive it and you're hooked.

British manufacturers had nothing with which to seriously compete either. Rolls-Royce continued to make the flabby and pedestrian Silver Shadow which, within less than two decades, woud be reduced to 'wedding car' status. As has already been noted Jaguar had the XJ6, but build quality and reliability problems prevented large exports of the car. Aston-Martin were engaged in making gas-guzzling gentlemen's chariots of fire, and Bristol continued with hand-built, noblemen's mechanical dinosaurs.

Italy had its exotica, mostly in the form of very expensive Ferraris, and Lamborghini's attempt at making a high-speed, four-seater Grand Tourer wasn't to everyone's liking. *Motor Sport*'s Denis Jenkinson tested an Espada in 1970 and noted, among other points, spots of rust bubbling through the paintwork!

Until the advent of the Maserati-engined Citroën SM in 1971, French manufacturers had nothing remotely resembling competition for BMW in this market. A staple diet of mundane Renault 16s, Citroen IDs and CXs, and Peugeot 404s provided transport for a nation that had invented motor racing, yet seemed more interested in sea, sand, *son et lumière* and sex.

For BMW the 2800CS represented a supreme technical achievemnt in 1969, but this was merely a beginning, as the 2.8-litre car provided the basis for further development. In time it would evolve into one of the best and most exciting driver's cars of all time.

THE BEST IS YET TO COME

In 2.8-litre form the big coupé was indeed a great machine, but BMW were well aware that it had a lot more potential, and started plans to modify it from a very early stage. The first major change to this basically sound design came in 1971, when the 2.8-litre power unit was enlarged to 3 litres and the car was consequently badged as the 3.0CS.

The increase in engine capacity to 2,985cc (182cu in) was achieved by widening the bore from 86mm to 89mm, but retaining the same 80mm stroke. In this revised form the engine developed 180bhp at 5,800rpm and 185lb/ft of torque at 3,500rpm. The compression ratio was reduced in the 2.8-litre from 9:1 to 8.3:1, in order that the engine could run on regular 91 octane fuel. Easily able to meet the demands of American emissions regulations by this time, the power unit was fed by a brace of Zenith 35/40 twin-choke carburettors.

Despite a tendency for these engines to suffer from cracked cylinder heads, due to excessive build-up of under-bonnet heat, this was one of the world's finest 'sixes', and one by which all others would be measured. A number of owners would eventually complain bitterly that the dual Zenith carburettors were overly complex and difficult to keep in tune, but there was always a solution on hand to solve this problem – a visit to an official BMW dealer. The days when home 'tinkering' with a screwdriver and other primitive hand tools in the confines of a dimly lit and cluttered garage, and listening for changes in the engine note before making adjustments, were well and truly over by the early 1970s. Do-it-yourself enthusiasts meddled at their peril.

Gear Change

The engine was mated directly to a Getrag 4-speed manual gearbox, which was a redesigned version of the original ZF unit. Criticism of the 2.8's gearbox was that the synchromesh could be beaten on fast upward changes, a problem that simply didn't exist in the modified design, although shifting became a little stiffer as a result. Again, such was the torque delivery of the engine that a 5-speed gearbox was not considered to be necessary.

Gear ratios were as follows: First 3.85:1, Second 2.20:1, Third 1.40:1, Fourth 1:1, Final-drive 3.64:1. A 3-speed automatic was available as an extra-cost option, and this version of the car was badged as the 3.0 CSA.

Improved Performance

The top speed of the revised car was an entirely respectable 133mph, as was a time of 8secs for the 60mph dash from standstill, but again it was the unflustered, quiet manner in which the coupé achieved such 'top-notch' performance. At this time there

The 180bhp 3-litre engine had a lower compression ratio to allow it to run on low octane fuel. Early units breathed through a brace of Zenith carburettors until fuel injection was perfected.

were plenty of Ferraris, Maseratis and Lamborghinis that were faster in a straight line – all quite capable of blowing the 'Bimmer' into the weeds – but these were out-and-out sports two-seaters. The BMW, despite its increased performance and bulk, was still a car that could be thrown nimbly around down country lanes.

Incidentally, right-hand drive versions, for the benefit of the few markets where the odd practice of driving on the 'wrong' side of the road was still the norm, were purpose-built rather than being conversions from left-hand drive.

Softening Up

Naturally, the suspension specification was the same as that of the 2.8-litre car, but was made softer for the benefit of Americans. The hard springing that had typified virtually all German cars down the years did not go down very well with those Americans who had been used to the softly suspended home-grown product. Stiffer springs and anti-roll bars were available to more sporting drivers, but at extra cost!

Responding to the Press

One of the biggest improvements was in the adoption of 10.7in vented, and power-assisted, disc brakes at all four corners. This gave a swept braking area of 493sq in, and vastly improved stopping power. The power-assisted worm-and-roller steering was also redesigned and had a more manageable 3.7 turns from lock to lock.

The same five-spoke cast-alloy wheels were fitted, but differed in that they were shod with a wider variety of tyres from market to market. In Britain and Europe there were wide 195/70 VR14 radials and 7in rims, while the Americans got 175 HR14 radials on 6in rims.

Criticism of the interior was never an issue, which is why the revised car was to the same sumptuous standard as previously. There was cord/cloth trim as standard and leather as an extra-cost option. Wood veneer was used for the dashboard and door cappings, the seat hinges were still chromed and there were stainless steel coverings for the sills and door jambs.

As the body had not been changed the view from the driver's seat was just the same as before. The large glass area, pillarless doors, large windscreen, nicely laid out instruments, and large diameter steering wheel all gave an aura of safety and solidity.

In Britain, the majority of customers plumped for the standard cloth upholstery. One of the author's favourite cars, the 3.0CSA is an all-time classic that still feels modern even by today's standards.

BMW 2800 Saloon (1968–77)

Layout and Chassis	Unitary construction, all-steel, four-door saloon

Engine

Type	In-line
Block material	Cast-iron with conventional water jackets
Head material	Light alloy
Cylinders	Six
Cooling	Water
Bore × stroke	86 × 80mm
Capacity	2,788cc
Valves	Two per cylinder
Timing	Single ohc
Compression ratio	9:1
Maximum power	192bhp (SAE) at 6,000rpm
Maximum torque	174lb ft at 3,700rpm
Fuel system	Twin Zenith 35/40 INAT carburettors
Fuel tank capacity	19.8gal (90ltr)

Gears

Gearbox	4-speed synchromesh
Ratios	First 3.85
	Second 2.08
	Third 1.38
	Fourth 1.00
	Final drive 3.45
Clutch	Single dry-plate

Suspension and steering

Front	Independent by MacPherson struts, coil springs and anti-roll bar
Rear	Independent by semi-trailing arms, coil springs and anti-roll bar
Steering	Power-assisted recirculating ball with 3.5 turns from lock to lock
Tyres	HR14 radial
Wheels	Vented pressed steel 14inx6in

Brakes

	Power-assisted discs front and rear

Dimensions (in/mm)

Track	Front 57/1,448
	Rear 58/1,473
Wheelbase	106/2,692
Overall length	185/4,699
Overall width	69/1,753
Overall height	57/1,448
Dry weight	2,954lb (1,340kg)

Performance

Maximum speed	124mph (200km/h)
0–60mph (0–100km/h)	8.8sec
fuel consumption	15–21mpg (13.5–18.9ltr × 100km)

What the press said

In Britain the 3.0CS came with a price tag of £5,345, and was well in excess of $10,000 in the United States. Those who thought this excessive, and there were several, were apt to compare the purchase price with that of Ferrari's stunningly beautiful Dino 246, which was in similar financial territory.

They argued along the lines of 'Why buy a BMW when you can buy a Ferrari for the same money?' The Ferrari had real charisma, was mid-engined, handled superbly and would almost top 150mph. On the flip side of the coin its 2.4-litre V6 engine suffered from poor 'top-end' lubrication, the car had only limited cabin and luggage space and bodywork that was notoriously prone to corroding.

Road & Track's Jonathan Thompson and many other journalists were easily able to justify the BMW's hefty purchase price. In June 1977 Thompson commented:

> I had the privilege and pleasure (I was nearly ecstatic, in fact) to drive one of the first 2800CS coupés in Munich in 1969. At that time I couldn't think of a better all-round car for both my needs and desires; in June 1972 when we did the 'Shapes That Worked' feature for our 25th anniversary issue it was still my favourite, both aesthetically and mechanically, and in many respects I still prefer the 2800/3.0CS to the latest 630CSi.

Autosport's John Bolster, whose respected opinion was objective and restrained in typically British style, was similarly enthusiastic about the new car. He described the revised gearbox as an absolute dream – 'the usual BMW 90mph in third gear' – praised the well spaced pedals and was especially impressed by the supple suspension. Having tested the car on some of France's roughest roads he commented:

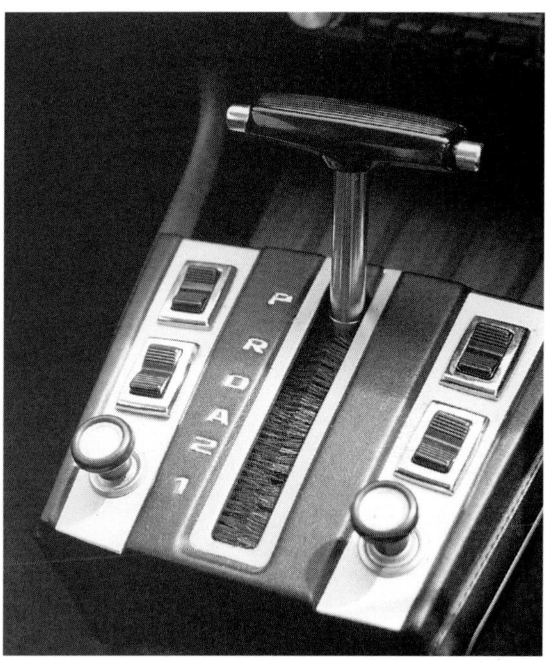

The 3.0CS's interior was to the same luxurious specification as the 2.8's. Automatic transmission was offered at extra cost, and was particularly popular in North America.

The appearance is not excessively sporting, which could attract unwelcome attention, but there is just the suggestion of speed and power about its lines which causes other road users to move over when the BMW appears in their mirrors.

This is precisely what BMW had set out to achieve – a conservative, unassuming 'express' to be appreciated by those who looked beneath the surface for hidden qualities. It is a policy that has been employed to this day. The 2800CS had been a good start in the league of big sporting 6-cylinder cars. The 3-litre had been an improvement, but further development would turn the coupé from a well-engineered sporting 'heavyweight' into one of the world's most outrageous driving machines.

Entirely functional, the dashboard continued with four main instruments – combination gauge, tachometer, speedometer and clock – but the wood veneer was not to Jaguar or Rolls-Royce standards.

Polished wheelarch 'clip-ons' have always been popular accessories and look extremely smart, but tend to trap moisture and hasten corrosion.

A SHOT IN THE HEAD

In 1972 the 3.0CS was superseded by the 3.0CSi, which had Bosch electronic fuel injection instead of twin Zenith carburettors. The latter were retained on automatic versions. The switch to fuel injection was a logical, if late, development. After all, Daimler-Benz had introduced fuel injection on the 300SL 'Gullwing' back in the 1950s and Triumph on the 2.5PI in 1967.

Its benefits of increased power, smoother running and more accurate fuel metering had been known for many years, but a few 'die-hards' including Ferrari had persisted with carburettors as they were much cheaper to produce. For BMW the switch to fuel injection came about because of the company's involvement in motor sport.

It meant extra power for the 3-litre engine, with which the racing versions could compete against powerful opposition from Ford of Cologne. Another benefit was that the car was more easily able to meet with exhaust emissions regulations in the United States. There was also more power available. The carburettor engine met with California's smog requirements, but its power output was strangled, as *Road & Track* noted in 1973.

The magazine commented:

The big BMW engine is without doubt the most sophisticated in-line six in the world and its sonority is very much part of the car's character. This year's tightened limit on oxides of nitrogen in the State of California has taken its toll, to be sure; fuel economy isn't what it used to be and the exhaust gas recirculation, plus retarded spark at low engine speeds render what was once a beautifully responsive engine somewhat reluctant in around-town work.

Fuel injection circumnavigated this problem in one fell swoop, and allowed for greater development of the 'hairy' racing versions. In roadgoing trim the engine developed 200bhp at 5,500rpm, although the seven-bearing crankshaft was perfectly safe up to 7,000rpm. The compression ratio was raised to 9.5:1, and BMW stuck rigidly to its policy of employing a single-overhead camshaft driven by the crankshaft.

Although Daimler-Benz had been the first to make a fuel-injected production petrol engine, it was Volkswagen who brought a reliable version to the mass market with the Type 4 saloons, and later the Beetle.

Modern 5-spoke alloy wheels are fitted to this concours CSA, and give the car an even more sporting look, even if purists disapprove.

On the road the CSA is powerful yet restful, and still makes for sensible luxury transport in the 1990s. This German-registered example is owned by Dr Ralph Schmidt and driven on a daily basis.

Electronic Jab

Dubbed L-jetronic in the BMW, the system measured air-flow accurately into the cylinder bores for the purpose of delivering the fuel/air mixture. A fuel pump governed by a pressure regulator dispensed fuel to each of the six injectors at a relatively low pressure of 40psi. Electronic sensors fed information about air flow, engine temperature and engine revs, and throttle opening position, to a central computer which governed precisely how much fuel was needed for a given situation.

Electronic pulses are sent directly to the injectors with the result that these opened and closed instantly depending on the engine's needs. Airflow that primarily determines the quantity and rate of fuel flow, is controlled by a flap valve in the inlet housing. The amount by which the valve pivots is picked up by a control sensor in the form of an electronic signal through the wonderfully named potentiometer.

The system is complex, of course, but its advantages won the day over carburettors almost universally by the 1980s. It was this system that really started the technical revolution in motor manufacturing in the late 1980s and early 1990s, and signalled the inevitable replacement of motor mechanics with highly qualified auto technicians.

With 200bhp available on tap the CSi was, by any standards of the day, extremely rapid. Top speed was in the region of 137mph and the car was capable of accelerating from rest to 60mph in 8secs. It is food for thought that the Mercedes-Benz 'Gullwing' of the mid-1950s, that had the same engine capacity and number of cylinders, was capable of 155mph and similar 0–60mph acceleration potential. This aside the BMW was about right for the era in which it was made.

Autosport's John Bolster described it as a 'real ball of fire', a 'car of dramatic performance' that had lost none of its smoothness and refinement. Considering its power output the car was also remarkably quiet. Jaguar's classic, but ageing in-line 6-cylinder engine that had powered both the saloons and sports cars since 1948 boasted an additional camshaft, but in terms of development was becoming pretty tired by 1973.

Performance figures for the 3.0CSi were typically 35mph in bottom gear, 60mph in second, 95mph in third and 137mph in top. An automatic gearbox was available at extra cost and, whereas ZF had been the chosen supplier for the previous carburettor model, a Borg-Warner unit was fitted to the fuel-injection cars. Both types were 3-speeders and entirely conventional in having a hydraulic torque converter and planetary gears. The automatics were equally refined, of course, but some 4mph slower at the top end of the speed range.

Naturally, this was wholly academic, but driving enthusiasts, particularly the younger ones, chose the 4-speed manual version. And, then, BMW delivered a further development of the manual car in the guise of the utterly fabulous 3.0CSL.

A SHARK IN SHARKS' SCALES

The CSL version (L for Lightweight) was almost, but not quite, the ultimate weapon on the 3.0CS theme. Retailing at £6,399 in Britain and DM31,950 in Germany, this was an expensive 140mph machine. Externally these quite stunningly presented cars were distinguishable from the standard ones by a black body stripe running on both sides of the bodywork above the 'waistline', bright mouldings, chromed wheelarch covers, a deep chin spoiler below the front bumper, multi-spoke alloy road wheels and 3.0CSL badges on both front wings and rear lid.

Lightweight aluminium-alloy body panels, including the doors and front and rear

In 1972 the CS was replaced by the fuel-injected CSi; externally, the only give-away was the revised badge on the rear lid.

BMW had gained a great deal of experience previously with the 4-cylinder fuel-injected 2002 Tii. The installation was neat, accessible for maintenance and worked well.

Fitted to the 6-cylinder engine, fuel injection increased power output to 200bhp, and gave BMW the opportunity to compete on the race tracks against the Cologne-built Ford Capris.

lids were fitted as standard, although, curiously, steel ones could be specified according to customer preference. To further reduce weight, the steel body pressings were made in a narrower-gauge steel than the standard cars.

In all there were just 1,039 of these fabulous machines made, and they held plenty of development potential. The car was intended as BMW's homologation special for Group 2 saloon car racing. Further modifications from standard included a limited-slip differential, a huge 17-gallon fuel tank and, to further reduce weight, most of the sound-proofing material employed in the regular car's body was removed.

Wood veneer continued to be used for the dashboard and door cappings, and the stock four-dial instrument panel was also retained. In 'standard' roadgoing form these cars were supplied with wide 195–70 VR14

Michelin XAX radial tyres which, crude as they were by today's standards, were considered as state-of-the-art rubberware during 1972 and 1973.

Curiously, BMW chose comparatively 'soft' suspension settings that not only gave acceptable ride quality, but were very much along the lines of contemporary German thinking. Ten years previously Daimler-Benz had launched the radical 230SL sports car. Chief development engineer, Rudi Uhlenhaut, had brought considerable pressure to bear on tyre companies to get their act together in coming up with a decent radial tyre. This they did, and Uhlenhaut put all his experience with the Grand Prix cars of the 1930s and 1950s into the 230SL. This included softer springing which, in conjunction with radial tyres, produced a comfortable handling package that none could equal.

With its comparatively small capacity 2.3-litre 6-cylinder engine, the 230SL was capable of little more than 125mph, but was as quick around a racing circuit as a Ferrari 250GT, as Uhlenhaut himself demonstrated so ably upon the car's press launch in 1963. BMW had cottoned on to the same basic idea.

The Pen is Mighty

In 1928 one of the great pioneering motorists, Charles Jarrot, wrote in his book *Ten Years of Motoring and Motor Racing*:

I have no copyright, no freehold in the road, and have no foolish ideas tending that way. But I do claim – more, believe – that then and now, from 1896 to 1906, and from 1906 onward, few ordinary men ever loved any

The 4-cylinder 2000s had provided BMW with track success in the late 1960s, and the inspiration to develop the 6-cylinder coupés for a similar role. These amazing machines would provide a portent of greater things ahead.

In every sense the CSi – this example is fitted with a deep chin spoiler – was an exciting driver's car with few real rivals. Only the Porsche 911 Carrera provided the same thrills above 120mph.

As a basis for homologation in international motor sport, BMW launched the 3.0CSL (L for Lightweight), which had alloy doors and front and rear lids.

personal thing as I loved and still love the never ending road.

It was this powerful passage that inspired *Motor Sport*'s editor Bill Boddy to undertake a truly epic journey in a 3.0CSL, writing of the experience in the January 1973 issue of his revered journal. Boddy, and photographer Michael Tee, undertook to visit ten European capital cities in four days. They included London, Paris, Monte-Carlo, Rome, Vienna, Bonn, Luxembourg, Brussels, Amsterdam and back to London.

We were away from Calais in this interesting car at 11.29 Continental time, heading for Dunkirk and the Autoroute to Paris. Already the sense of freedom one feels as soon as France is entered was apparent, as we made good time under a cloudy sky.

A Grand Tour in a Grand Touring car had begun.

Cruising at 5,900rpm the car headed south at a gentlemanly 130mph – a speed the car was to hold for the best part of four days.

So here we were in this excellent motor car, going at more than 130mph, with church spires spiking the sparse, flat landscape, under a sky of the faintest blue, a painter's paradise no doubt, but for us merely fleeting scenery flanking the rapidly-unfolding ribbon of the A1 autoroute beyond Lille.

Between London and Monte-Carlo, a distance of 891 road miles, time had been taken out to cross the English Channel and dine in Paris, but the journey had taken just 17 hours and 2 minutes. The car had averaged a breathtaking 75mph. Charles Jarrott

Despite the massive increase in engine power and torque, the CSi retained the restrained elegance and gait of the original 2.8-litre carburettor car.

had accomplished the same journey in 1906 aboard a 7-litre Crossley in 37.5 hours, largely a reflection on France's roads during the early part of the century.

As Boddy pointed out, Dudley Noble's 2-litre Rover Light Six had beaten the 'Blue Train' from St Raphael to Calais by 20 minutes in 1930 and had averaged 44mph. The great Woolf Barnato completed the long sojourn in his Speed-Six Bentley from Cannes to Boulogne at an average of 43.43mph, but Bill Boddy considered the task of running the BMW against France's express trains as pointless – train travel was much faster than any car on the congested roads of Europe.

Boddy's journey continued ever onwards. 'Our only meal since breakfast in Monte-Carlo,' he wrote, 'was taken in Bolzano, a dreary town in the winter gloom, full of poor cafés and not a Frazer Nash in sight.' This was a fitting, if typically eccentric Boddy comment; Frazer Nash's connections with BMW went back a long way.

Distinguished by their side stripes and CSL badging, the lightweights were expensive to buy and run, and total production ran out after 1,039 examples had found enthusiastic owners.

Before sinking into oblivion I reflected that the CSL was going as well as ever, inspite of having been held at 5,000–6,000rpm almost continuously and that even in the dark it had blown off a Porsche 914 and the very occasional Citroën SM.

During heavy rain and blizzard conditions encountered in Austria, Boddy and Tee were treated to the advantages of the big, ventilated disc brakes and meaty radial tyres. It's interesting that Boddy commented:

I was reminded that tyre regulations were strictly enforced in these parts, cars on cross-ply tyres having to carry a 100 k.p.h. maximum speed sign on their back windows, which made us conscious of the splendid grip our Michelin XAXs had on all kinds of slippery surfaces. Through one blizzard, incidentally, the speed of the CSL was reduced to 100mph for safety's sake!

The total mileage covered on this journey worked out at 3,789 miles, much of it at well over 100mph. Apart from periodic top-ups with engine oil, a momentary loss of engine power and a brief period of trouble with the windscreen wipers, the car remained trouble-free throughout.

Considering the high cruising speeds, an average of 15.13mpg and 950 miles per pint of oil was deemed reasonable. Boddy noted:

Its top speed timed against kilometre posts in the Po Valley (Italy) proved to be 146mph at 6,500rpm with the speedometer reading 140mph. The best hour was 127.4 miles on the wet autoroute south of Paris during the first day.

Boddy, whose opinion was usually delivered in an objective manner, rated the car extremely highly. 'Far from being a "rorty racer", this is a refined fast car of very great

Aggressive and sure-footed, a well-driven CSL provided for sensational motoring in 1973. Despite the march of technology these cars have lost none of their unique appeal.

An extravagant Grand Tourer, the CSL provided Bentley Continental road manners but with the advantage of Porsche performance.

Like so many BMWs, CSLs are happiest on a racing circuit like these in the pits at Silverstone at a club test day.

High-speed sojourns on the track with these cars demonstrated aerodynamic instability; the slim dorsal spoilers on the front wings went a long way to eradicating recalcitrant handling traits.

performance. It is well balanced but not harshly sprung,' he noted. His only criticism was the lack of a fifth gear and a certain amount of 'axle tramp' under violent acceleration away from rest. His test car was fitted with an experimental chin spoiler at the front that Boddy claimed helped greatly with front-wheel adhesion.

And, despite heavy use of the brakes when slowing down to negotiate slower traffic, tyre wear, considering the speed and mileage, was negligible. Boddy measured precisely that 1.3mm of tread had worn on the front offside, 1.1mm on the front inside, 3.2mm on the rear offside and 2.8mm on the rear onside. All four tyres had started the journey with a depth of 9.5mm. This was the kind of attention to detail that set *Motor Sport* aside from the herd.

Boddy and Tee's journey was a grand journey in a modern age on crowded roads. He remarked:

> The CSL confirms the well-known fact that BMW have scarcely made a bad car and it

Among the most coveted and valuable of all BMWs, restoring a CSL to this condition is expensive, time-consuming and generally painful, but certainly worthwhile.

must enhance enormously the prestige of the entire present day range. The CSL made no bones about running close to its top speed for hours on end.

As an aside, a Frazer Nash BMW 328 put 101 miles into an hour at the Brooklands track in 1937!

Boddy had made his point; the cars and roads of Europe were fast, both making for high-speed travel between cities. BMW had made a particularly efficient machine for this purpose, but a car that also doubled as a racing machine. This Grand Touring/racing ethic prevailed at the time, or at least until the oil crisis killed them off. Cars for the well-heeled were not in short supply. In the CSL BMW arguably made the best of them.

Boddy concluded:

> So much for this pocket Grand Tour. In the eighteenth and nineteenth centuries it would have lasted more than seven months and cost some £420. A well known motoring writer has said that twelve years ago it could have been done in seven weeks, at half the cost. We did ours in four days, for rather less, but perhaps the tourists did a trifle more sightseeing!

From the 'Batcave'

In its standard early form, the CSL was an exciting sports tourer with purposeful lines that created something of an impression, even in the company of exotica from Italy. However, at very high speeds, the Karmann-built body was shown to be wanting in aerodynamic stability. The answer to this was a revised car nicknamed the 'Batmobile'. This was a quite outrageous machine that started something of a revolution in aerodynamic devices as fitted to roadgoing cars.

Nicknamed the 'Batmobile', a small number of special road versions of the CSL were built with front, rear and roof-mounted aerofoils. Despite the wing badges, this example is actually a 3.2-litre car.

One of the most outrageous road cars ever built, Batmobiles appear to go like stink whether they're being driven or not.

The huge rear wing was similar in effect to the 'ducktail' spoiler employed on contemporary Porsches, and promoted downforce over the rear wheels where it was most needed.

Although built in 1973, the only items to date these cars are the tall-profile tyres. Tyre manufacturers were clearly behind chassis development, which is why these fabulous machines can be made to slide at will in corners.

A Batmobile with BBS cross-spoke alloy wheels and modern low-profile rubber may appear odd to some . . .

. . . but this combination improves track adhesion almost out of recognition.

A full-width chin spoiler was fitted at the front and the bumper was dispensed with altogether. Longitudinal, straked fins were attached on top of the front wings, there was a radical aerofoil along the trailing edge of the roof panel and another raised wing mounted on two longitudinal 'tailplanes' on top of the rear wings.

These 'strange' appendages created a great deal of controversy and were eventually banned in Germany. A fundamental lack of understanding prevailed among the traffic authorities in this otherwise enlightened bastion of engineering know-how. High-speed stability was one of the decisive factors in adding these wind-tunnel proven devices, but the other was the little-understood concept of 'downforce'.

Naturally, it had been known for many years that atmospheric pressure on body-work had the effect of slowing a car down. Engine power could overcome this to a certain extent, but in harnessing airflow more successfully, BMW (and Porsche) quickly discovered that more grip could be obtained from the tyres by dint of greater air pressure being artificially forced onto the rear wing.

In 1973 this science was in its infancy. More than 25 years later, despite the expenditure of millions by racing car manufacturers and others, aerodynamic theory often remains at variance with practice. The Batmobile, incidentally, spurred Porsche to develop ever wilder versions of the racing 911s. They weren't pretty, but the speed at

The classic 30CS was replaced in the mid-1970s by the 6 series cars, with engines ranging from 2.8 to 3.5 litres. Again, this was a full four-seater and had superb road manners, but the styling was suggestive of middle-aged 'spread'.

The quickest and most collectable of the 6 series breed, the M6 incorporated race-bred technology from the 3.0CS racing cars.

The mighty in-line 6-cylinder 3.5-litre M6 engine was undoubtedly one of BMW's best-ever power units, but cost plenty to run.

THE SIX-CYLINDER SALOONS

With the 2800CS and 3.0CS cars, which began life in 1968, BMW had clearly set their sights on gaining a share of a market largely occupied by the Porsche 911 and Mercedes-Benz 280SL sports car. It was a lucrative, if relatively small sector, and would not have sustained the company's prosperity alone.

Launched and developed concurrently with the sporting coupés were the big saloons in the form of the 2500 and 2800. These handsome cars were designed to attack the Jaguar and Merc executive class. In time they would be developed into what would be widely acknowledged as the world's best all-round saloon car – the 525i.

Helmut Bonsch, BMW's marketing director once stated:

> The world knows that Mercedes-Benz invented the motor car. When a man makes good in business here he immediately thinks of a Mercedes. We want to give him a choice. If he likes to drive and wants performance more than he wants the Mercedes name he'll buy a BMW. Mercedes is living on its reputation!

These were harsh, and not wholly accurate sentiments, but indicative of BMW's clear purpose, direction and aggressive marketing strategy.

The 2500/2800 cars were conceived as roomy versions of the 2002. They weren't sporting in the same way as the CS coupés, although an enthusiastic driver at the wheel of one of these fine machines always had a lot of fun, but had performance aplenty in a sober heavyweight. It was the kind of car that would appeal to a successful professional or businessman in the over-40s age group.

From the pretty 2.0CS of the mid-60s to the 6 series (foreground) of the 1970s and beyond, BMW coupés have always been special, distinctive and accorded almost instant classic status.

which technology developed as a result certainly proved their worth.

It's interesting that relatively low-powered cars, like the pre-War BMW 328, which developed 80bhp from the 2-litre straight six, could easily accomplish a speed of 115mph. This was due in part to the aerodynamic slippery body. Such cars were capable of penetrating their air very efficiently. What the winged cars of the modern era had, though, was both straight-line speed and the ability to travel round corners at a hitherto unknown rate.

Batmobiles were fast – 150mph top speed was easily on the cards – and loosely formed the basis of BMW's fabulous track racing car.

Sharing the same bodyshell, the 2500 and 2800 models were 8in longer than the 1600–2000 range, and had a 6in longer wheelbase. Aesthetically, the Munich parentage was readily apparent. Up front was a chromed kidney grille, with horizontal bars right and left and twin headlamps.

Elegant chromed bumpers were fitted front and rear – overriders were optional in some markets – and, in contrast to so many cars, they weren't overly large. So many manufacturers had a tendency in this era to cater for ham-fisted types, whose ability to park in tight spaces was often notable for sickening thumps and thuds into cars fore and aft, by fitting massive, ugly bumpers.

There was the characteristic large glass area, four doors, huge boot and Germanically attractive rectangular rear lamps. Bright mouldings were fitted around the perimeter of the windows, but not along the sides of the body at 'waist level'. Here, a prominent and attractive swage line was deemed sufficient to break the large expanse of sheet metal. Bright trim was considered to be unnecessary and superfluous. Paint finish and panel fit were outstanding.

In contrast to the coupés' attractive alloy wheels, the saloons had 6×14 steel disc wheels (shod with Michelin XAS 175HR 14 radial tyres), closed by chromed hubcaps – BMW roundels at their centres – and vented alloy rim trims.

The 6-cylinder 2500 and 2800 saloon range was launched in 1968–69 as direct competition to the stolid saloons from Daimler-Benz.

This was a large car yet the stylists had put a good deal of thought into detailing, and it didn't appear to have the ungainly weight of some of its peers.

Safety First

Both primary and secondary safety played central roles in the car's design, areas in which German engineers clearly led other nations. The all-steel bodyshell – steel was also used for the doors and front and rear lids – was, of course, on the unitary construction principle and 30 per cent stiffer in torsional rigidity than the mid-range 2000 model.

This was BMW's first venture into the world of rigid central passenger cells, with the front and rear ends designed to fold and collapse in the unfortunate event of a collision. Safety was of prime importance because these big, luxury saloons were designed for high speed.

As one of BMW's senior engineers, Helmut Bonsch, once pointed out: 'Driving is a fast game, and we must have the right car in which to enjoy the game and play it safely.'

Bonsch was absolutely right. By the late 1960s and early 1970s the roads of Europe – particularly the motorway network – had changed almost out of recognition. High speeds were possible over long distances, largely thanks to manufacturers like BMW and Daimler-Benz.

In 1973, a journey from Paris to Lyons in France on the motorway brought home forcefully to this author what fast driving was about. Each lane of the autoroute on that dark, exciting evening was crowded with cars travelling 'bumper-to-bumper' at very high speed. For one car in the pack to have slowed down would have been to court certain disaster, and cause a pile-up of hideous magnitude.

The fast boys in the outside lane were easily nudging 120mph, and comprised the S-Class Mercs, Citroën SMs, an occasional Ferrari and a number of BMWs. There was a never-ending stream of them, clearly breaking every speed regulation in the book. The police were utterly helpless. The cars could not be stopped or slowed down. This was clearly a race to the south of France; inter-marque rivalry was self-evident. At one juncture a maroon-coloured 2800, driven by an impatient maniac, cut across from the outside lane and charged down the hard shoulder at unabated speed in an attempt to get ahead.

It was a piece of adrenalin-pumping madness – definitely not to be encouraged – but that was completely wonderful to witness. But this was the early 1970s when the concept of personal freedom was often achieved without duty, and motor car manufacturers had to cater, in terms of safety, for the people who had little respect for the consequences of their actions. The big BMW saloons were designed to be driven fast but, at the same time, were also immensely safe.

A DIFFERENT VIEW

The Rover driving editor of *Motor Sport*, Bill Boddy, tested a 2500 early in its career, and was suitably impressed, but summed up perfectly the reasons why the British, in particular, should welcome this German machine. He wrote:

This elegant and spacious BMW arrived at an opportune moment in my motoring life, in as much as the faithful and much-liked leather-upholstered editorial Rover 2000TC, in which both dogs ride, had become somewhat long in the tooth, sluggish, with a boot-lid all too ready to fly open even when

A fast sports machine with handsome looks, Munich's cruisers served as almost unrivalled inter-city 'expresses', and paved the way for the legendary 5 series cars of the modern era.

locked, a loose hand-brake grip, undependable starting, and front suspension which all too rapidly wore illegal flats on the outer extremities of the front tyres.

Boddy's, regrettably, was an all too familiar yarn. He went on:

It was due for replacement anyway and I favoured a Rover 3500V8 but due to the inability of Solihull to let me try a manual transmission version, either for road test or as potential customer, over a period of five months, the matter is in abeyance. So I was all set to become BMW minded . . .

This was yet another indictment of the ailing British motor industry.

INSIDE STORY

Road & Track described the styling of the 2500/2800 range as requiring 'little comment'. The writer of the May 1969 report remarked: 'It is clean and tasteful, making no demands on the car's function, but one also wonders if it could be more eye-catching while still meeting these criteria.'

No matter what anyone thought of the looks – and owners went for these cars largely because of the way they looked – the package as a whole was one of competence, and acceptable standards of luxury and comfort that had been lacking from so many saloons.

A full five-seater, the interior design was again typically functional and practical. The seat covers were in hard-wearing fluted vinyl, or cloth, with matching door panels, and leather was an extra-cost option. The floorpan was, of course, fully carpeted.

The instruments and controls were similar in layout to those of the coupé model. In front of the driver was a large-diameter, three-spoke steering wheel straight from the Munich parts bin. As power-assisted steering was standard, this size of wheel appeared to be ridiculous to most. Like the coupé's, the dashboard was 'stepped' to provide useful storage space on the lower flat surface. Swivelling fresh air vents were provided on the outer extremities of the dashboard, with the controls for the heating system on the central console above the radio set. In front of the centrally positioned gear lever, the stubby gear shifter was shrouded neatly in a rubber boot.

It would have saved the company a great deal of money if the coupé's instrument cluster had been utilized but, being more sporting, it didn't quite fit in with the saloon's image, and the latter's was therefore made to a fresh design. Contained within a hooded binnacle, the four instruments were circular, and black-faced with white characters. The speedometer sat to the left and the tachometer (red-lined at 6,200rpm) to the right with the comparatively small engine temperature and fuel gauge in the centre. A smaller panel containing the various warning lights sat below these two smaller instruments.

The instrument cluster gave adequate information and, thanks to the huge area of space between the steering wheel spokes, there was never a problem in reading the gauges. But stylish it wasn't. Some commentators even criticized the lack of markings between the main numerical divisions.

Road & Track reckoned that 'a driver couldn't ask for a more convenient instrument panel', but severely criticized some of the switchgear and door locks for being too small.

The vast majority of these cars led exceptionally hard lives, particularly on the European motorway network, and are rare today, even at club gatherings.

Car & Driver's Patrick Bedard on the other hand remarked: 'Each of the controls is perfectly direct, giving the impression of a car with no secrets.'

Whether behind the steering wheel or in the passenger seat, the BMW may not have the most stylish of luxury car interiors but, above all, it felt special. The seats were not only comfortable and gave plenty of support in the right places, but were also capable of massaging aches and pains away which, in conjunction with the generous noise damping materials employed around the body, made for most relaxing travel.

THE 2.5-LITRE SIX

During the late 1960s a 2.5-litre engine, and particularly one with six cylinders, was roughly a litre larger than a power unit in an average family saloon. Everyone in Europe, from engineers to the car buying public, considered an engine above 2-litre capacity to be a large one. The Americans didn't, of course, because they had become accustomed to V8s with 5- and 7-litre capacities.

The main difference between European and American engines, apart from several miles to the gallon, was that the former produced more power with fewer cubic inches. The BMW 2.5-litre unit was no exception to this general rule. Like all BMW sixes this unit was the engineering equivalent of a highly polished jewel.

With a bore and stroke of 86mm×71.6mm the overall capacity worked out at 2,494cc (152cu in) and, with a compression ratio of 9:1, maximum power of 170bhp was developed at 6,000rpm, with maximum torque of

Unfortunately, many of these grand old cars are languishing in scrapyards, but make for interesting restoration projects.

176lb/ft being pushed out at 3,700rpm. The unique combustion chamber design of the CS coupé was naturally utilized for both the 2.5-litre and 2.8-litre engines. The turbulence producing spherical structure around the sparking plugs and valves, and the 'humped' piston tops, enabled the engine to meet the American exhaust emissions laws at an output of 68bhp per litre without the need for an air pump. The design was exceptionally clever, and more important, it worked.

Naturally, the cylinder head was to a two-valve-per-cylinder format, and there was a single-overhead camshaft driven by duplex chain from the crankshaft. By this stage this was BMW's normal practice. But there was a newly designed type of water thermostat for this engine. BMW had 'twigged' that conventional thermostats control water arriving from the water jackets in the cylinder block.

In the depths of a typically cold European winter this returning water can, in some circumstances, be exceptionally cold, in effect fooling the thermostat as to its true temperature, resulting in cracked cylinder blocks. This unhappy problem was solved with a double-sided thermostat that responded also to water from the radiator, and reduced its flow in exceptionally cold conditions. For high operating temperatures the cooling system was aided by a viscous fan.

Fuel was dispensed to the cylinder bores through a brace of Solex 35/40 INAT carburettors fitted with automatic chokes.

Performance Rating

This wasn't the quickest saloon in its class, but again the 6-cylinder engine was acknowledged as one of the smoothest and most responsive to be found anywhere. Accelerating hard up through the gears, one of its most notable and endearing characteristics was the classic rasping noise from the exhaust that, in some ways, wasn't dissimilar to that of the Porsche 911.

For a relatively heavy car the 0–60mph sprint of 10sec was impressive, and maximum speed in each gear at 6,200rpm, more so. Typically they were: First 30mph, Second 57mph, Third 88mph and Fourth 118mph. *Road & Track*'s early assessment of the engine noted it for its quietness, but there was criticism. They commented:

At low speed it belies its modest 2.5 liter displacement with surprisingly generous torque and flexibility, but out on the freeway it sounds much too busy in spite of the easy going 3.54:1 final drive . . . .

The report continued:

In through-the-gears acceleration the 2500 is as impressive to the clocks as it is to the ear, producing quarter-mile times that many self-respecting Detroit engineers would say can't be done with 2.5 liters, 3000lb and tractability. And, like all BMWs, the 2500 is designed to run all day at its maximum speed . . . it seems to get into its stride only above the usual speed limits in America.

Car & Driver's testers managed to squeeze the 0–60mph time down to less than 9sec, and praised the German engineering know-how for extracting so much power from such 'small' cylinders. Patrick Bedard commented:

Detroit would say the engine was lavishly expensive and point an accusing finger at the cast aluminium oil pan held on by no less than three dozen bolts. At BMW engines are too expensive only if they don't work.

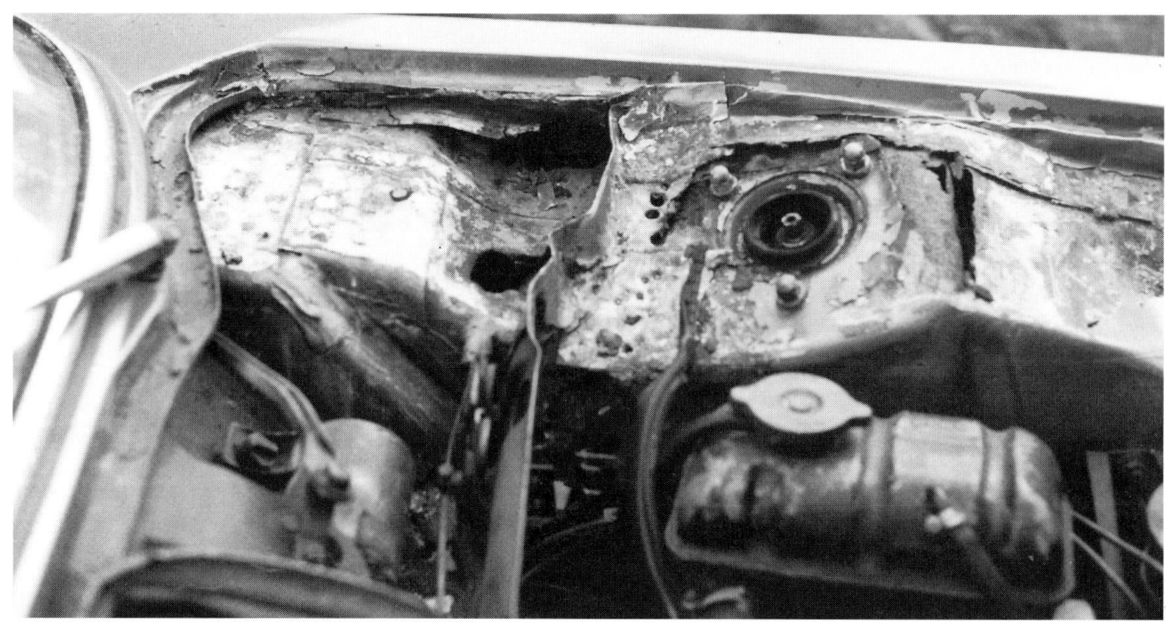

Tackling extensive rust in the inner wings and elsewhere is both expensive and time-consuming, but most definitely to be encouraged.

This point really summed up the huge difference between the mass-production car world of the United States – and elsewhere – and BMW's admirable attempts to produce quality engineering at a price that could be afforded by the affluent middle classes.

Bill Boddy of *Motor Sport*, whose test car required 'running in' during his time with it, was also impressed by the 2500, although he had cause to condemn the lack of power in the headlamps, and didn't think a great deal of the gear lever knob falling off in his hand.

As ever Boddy was apt to compare BMWs with equivalent British cars and commented:

Comparing the BMW with the Rover 3500 V8 I was so keen to try, the latter has an out-dated, cramped bodyshell, seating four only, and over-complicated suspension, and inspite of having 1,000cc more swept volume in its Buick-crib engine than the German car, is not all that much of a better performer – equal perhaps on speed, but more accelerative by only one fifth sec or so in the 0–60mph bracket, they tell me!

With the ability to return a good honest 20mpg-plus, the BMW was a good deal less thirsty than the products of Detroit and the Rover 3500 V8, the latter burning gas at the rate of between 15–17mpg in normal driving circumstances.

Transmission

In place of the Porsche-type synchromesh gearbox used in the 4-cylinder cars, the 2500 had a 4-speed Borg-Warner unit with the following ratios: First 3.85:1, Second 2.12:1, Third 1.38:1, Fourth 1:1. There is little doubt that the car was crying out for a fifth gear to allow for more relaxed cruising, but this 'tweak' wouldn't come as standard equipment on a BMW for several more years to come.

According to many journalists the Borg-Warner gearbox was light in use, although a little more 'notchy' than the Porsche system, but had the advantage over the latter in that bottom could be selected more easily without baulking. This baulking has been a feature of Porsche-designed gearboxes for many years, but it was a small price to pay for its inherent longevity and unrivalled reliability. Automatic transmission was an extra-cost option.

The 9.4in diaphragm clutch was also light in use, requiring little pedal pressure and the power-steering similarly needed very little effort. Both of these facets were intentionally dialled in by the designers. Heavy controls were not needed in an executive saloon despite its sporting nature. It was a car intended to offer stress-free motoring.

On the downside the power-steering was considered by many to be too light, and gave little feel of the road. This was one point about which American journalists were vociferous. Vague steering, they argued, was a feature of virtually all mid-range executive cars from Detroit. It is not something they expected from BMW.

Central Bank Balance

Like the 4-cylinder BMWs the front and rear suspension was to a now familar design layout. MacPherson struts were located in the bow, along with lower A arms, coil springs, hydraulic shock absorbers and an anti-roll bar, while semi-trailing arms, coil springs and telescopic dampers were used at the rear.

Despite the extra weight and larger dimensions (over and above the 4-cylnder cars), the 2500's handling characteristics largely mirrored the 2002's. The larger saloon was confidently sure-footed, forgiving of the most idiotic driver input, and safe. There was, however, a definite knack required in getting the best out of it. As Hans-Joachim Stuck later demonstrated with the racing Batmobile coupés, these saloons also needed to be picked up by the seat of the pants in a truly aggressive manner, and kicked around hard. Only when a driver felt brave enough to do this would the chassis respond crisply and neatly. In normal driving, though, it was just like any other well-honed 'super' saloon – unflustered, quiet, supple and a trifle dull.

Road & Track described the car's handling as 'exemplary' and added:

> There's lots of cornering power (even more is available with the optional D70–14 tires) and a just-right balance of generally neutral handling with slight power-off oversteer. Rough surfaces bring out the expected BMW suspension suppleness and utter lack of body flexing or rattling – we're afraid chassis like this make us hyper critical of more ordinary efforts. Two problems typical of BMW's semi-trailing arm rear suspension remain in the 2500 – wheel patter on brutal clutch engagement and inside wheel lifting on hard cornering – neither of which is a serious problem. The wheel patter only occurs in acceleration tests, and the lifting puts a relatively innocent limit on cornering activities.

As always these wheel-lifting antics were largely academic. The vast majority of BMW drivers would never experience this, as the speed needed in a corner to lift a wheel off the ground, was well beyond the capabilities and nerve threshold of normal mortals.

Bill Boddy of *Motor Sport* reckoned to feel completely at home in the corners, as he discovered that fast bends could be taken without anxiety. He commented:

> Its ZF power steering, with a taxi lock, and the smooth urge, even under breaking-in limitations, enables it to out-accelerate lesser cars out of bends, having gained yards on them by the tenacity of the grip of its Michelin-shod wheels going through them.

A jot of criticism, though. Boddy added: 'I'm not sure that I like the balance of the car on sudden corners.'

It's interesting that in modern times a number of BMW enthusiasts have restored these cars, and fitted them with the latest low-profile tyres. Thus equipped, they handle almost every bit as well as the current 5 Series range, a point that illustrates just how much the tyre manufacturers were dragging their feet during the 1960s.

Unsticking this big Bee-em from the road surface was a simple matter of changing down a cog or two, and stamping hard on the throttle pedal, at which juncture the tail-end would flick nicely out of line. There was nothing unusual in this, and in true BMW fashion, all that was required, once out of shape, was a shift on the steering wheel – a tad of opposite lock – and everything straightened out nicely. Lift-off oversteer was certainly a possibility, but anyone who experienced this – and some were sufficiently brave to admit publicly that they had – would have done well to have taken a course in driving tuition.

Power Harness

German-made ATE 10.7in-diameter disc brakes were fitted all round and power assisted. The handbrake worked on separate cast-iron drums cast integrally with the rear hubs. Stopping power was in the state-of-the-art category, with few systems to equal it, and few found fault with the car's stopping power.

Road & Track commented:

> Braking is nearly as impressive as handling; correct proportioning allows a deceleration rate of 0.77g on dry pavement with excellent directional control, and our standard fade test failed to produce a trace of fade though there was some pulling to the left. In everyday use the 2500 brakes are smooth, usually free of squeal and neither under- nor over-assisted by the vacuum unit.

Dependable All-Rounder at a Price

The 2500 gave the sporting driver a four-door, five-seater family saloon with ample luggage-carrying capacity, with an engine and chassis that could not be quite matched by Daimler-Benz. The car was an example of BMW drawing on all its antecedent experience to produce a 'top-drawer' piece of equipment straight out of the bag.

There were no bugs to be ironed out, no going back to the drawing board, and journalists on both sides of the Atlantic queued up to sing its virtues.

Although expensive to buy it was competitively priced. The basic list price in the United States was a cool $5,284. Air-conditioning, leather upholstery, automatic transmission and a radio bumped the price up to over $6,000. At this, American writers considered it to be good value. In Britain the car retailed at a tad over £3,000.

At the same time a 4.2-litre Jaguar XJ6 retailed at £2,937, the Rover 3500 V8 at £2,096 or the older style Rover 3.5-litre at £2,627. The Jaguar appeared to offer the best value among these esteemed carriages.

Here in long-wheelbase guise, the 3-litre version was almost as quick as the 3.0CS coupé and, unusually for a large car, boasted of handling to match.

The passage of time would prove otherwise. The late Michael Sedgwick, one of Britain's most celebrated car historians once remarked that he had once refused to inspect the underside of a Jaguar for fear of catching tetanus, a particularly nasty infection that could be contracted through contact with rusty metal.

Both types of Rover were cheaper than the BMW, but these stolid carriages were heavy, cumbersome and grossly out of date. And they certainly lacked appeal to sporting drivers. BMW were pushing saloon car frontiers. In some respects the Mercedes-Benz 280SE 3.5-litre V8 was arguably a better car but, as Bill Boddy noted: 'It should be, for it exceeds the cost of the BMW 2500 by no less than £2,159.'

Of the BMW Bill Boddy concluded:

Thus, all in all, the BMW 2500 seems an excellent proposition for those buying the lower echelon of luxury motor car – a Rolls-Royce Silver Shadow, which I readily admit is in a most worthy niche of its own, is £6,878 more costly, just to provide a sense of proportion.

Boddy omitted to note, though, that in 1968 when the BMW 2500 was launched, the Silver Shadow's chief overseer, Harry Grylls, retired. This great engineer then chose to buy a Volkswagen Beetle in which to enjoy his final motoring years.

Road & Track's conclusion was much the same as everyone else's. The BMW cost a lot of money but it was a price worth paying for top-quality engineering. 'There's no doubt,' they stated, 'that its performance is faster, more sporting and longer-legged than that of its nearest competitors.'

THE 'TWO EIGHT'

The 2800 version, or 'Two-eight' as it was sometimes known, was virtually identical to the 2500, except for the larger-capacity engine in the front. With its 86mm bore – the same as the 2500's – and 80mm stroke, over-all capacity was 2,788cc. Maximum power of 190bhp was developed at 6,000rpm, and maximum torque of 174lb/ft came in at 3,200rpm. This was, naturally, the same in-line 6-cylinder overhead-camshaft engine as used in the 2800CS.

Although more powerful than the 2.5-litre engine, and able to propel the car up to and beyond 125mph, the former power unit was the more satisfactory of the two in this chassis. The 2800 had bucketloads of torque, the ability to sprint from 0–60mph in under 9sec, but spirited driving, which was part of the point of owning one of these cars, produced fuel mileage figures that were occasionally dire. A high speed thrash across Europe could see sub-15mpg consumption. The well-off were probably not bothered by this; the Green movement that emerged in the 1970s most certainly was and manufacturers like BMW would be eventually forced to mend their ways.

ATTACKING MEASURES

In 1968 BMW manufactured no fewer than 116,000 cars, a mere drop in the ocean by comparison with the 'big boys' like Ford, Opel and Volkswagen, but the company was thriving nevertheless. It had established a

good reputation and one that was growing quickly, but it came apparent that, within a couple of years of launching the 2500/2800 cars, BMW's threat to Daimler-Benz just wasn't happening.

BMW's sales increased by roughly 10 per cent annually, but the Stuttgart concern – Munich's main competitor in the luxury class – was also selling cars in ever increasing numbers. Helmut Bonsch's view that Mercedes were living on a reputation had been misjudged and naive. The people who had invented the motor car certainly weren't going to capitulate to a 'new' pretender in the fold, no matter how good its products, and BMW were forced to think again.

The company's most important export market, North America, had taken well to the big saloons and coupés, but many had yet to be convinced of owning a 'badge' with a blue and white aeroplane propeller, instead of the hallowed three-pointed star.

THE BAVARIAN

Three years after the launch of the 6-cylinder saloons, BMW attacked the American market with the Bavaria model. Roughly one-sixth of BMW's total production output was exported to the United States and, in the over $5,000 category, Daimler-Benz were riding high. The Bavaria model was a clever marketing attempt to overcome the Merc supremacy.

The car was a mixed bag of 2500/2800 parts with the 2.8-litre engine. It was sold at a whisker under the psychologically daunting watershed price of $5,000. At this Daimler-Benz hadn't got a car capable of competing, and nor had any of the big Detroit manufacturers.

Car & Driver pointed out that the closest any car maker came to the Bavaria was

Volvo with their 3-litre, in-line 6-cylinder 164 model but this, the magazine commented, 'strayed too far to the "luxury" and away from the "sport" to be a real threat to Munich'.

The Bavaria, therefore, was a clever marketing ploy, the first in a long line of similar exercises aimed at both Daimler-Benz, and the original masters of such 'jiggery-pokery', the Americans. Externally the car was little different from its European-spec sisters, except that it had an alloy moulding along the flanks at 'waist level', which did nothing to improve the car's looks, and a Bavaria badge on the tail. The interior was from the standard 2500 and had Skai-vinyl seat covers. Leather upholstery was not an option.

Of the interior *Car & Driver* commented:

It's by no means stark, though there's nothing terribly rich about it. The individual front seats are firm in the typical German manner and likely to be comfortable over the long term; they offer little side support, so one must rely on the 3-point belts for that!

Tinted window glass, air-conditioning, alloy wheels similar to the ones fitted to the coupé, and power-assisted steering were all available as extra-cost options.

The combination of deeply supportive seats and leather upholstery gave 3-litre devotees supreme comfort in which to enjoy the 'ultimate driving experience'.

The regular 2.8-litre engine had a 9:1 compression ratio and a pair of twin-choke Zenith 38/40 INAT carburettors. The Borg-Warner 4-speed manual transmission was fitted and had the following ratios: first 3.85:1, second 2.08:1, third 1.38:1, fourth 1:1, final-drive ratio 3.64:1. (The standard 2800 had a final-drive ratio of 3.45:1).

Car & Driver recorded a best 0–60mph time of 8.7secs and a top speed of 124mph. The standard quarter-mile from rest was accomplished in a best of 16.4secs and such was the torque of the engine that the car would accelerate all the way to maximum speed from 15mph in top gear. There is little merit in actually performing this 'trick', but contemporary journalists considered it to be a 'pass mark' with large capacity 6-cylinder cars

Car & Driver described the Bavaria as 'one of the few high-performance imported cars that is comfortable in all driving conditions'. This was the 'no frills' 2800. Despite this there were luxury touches, such as the pull-down armrest in the centre of the rear seat, a fully carpeted boot, and the toolkit on the underside of the rear lid, so to own one of these cars – basic as it might have been – wasn't exactly 'slumming it'.

In launching it, though, BMW had the potential for shooting itself in the foot. *Car & Driver* commented:

All in the Bavaria is an incredibly good deal that should easily help BMW in its project to become a significant factor in the US marketplace. The only drawback we can see is what the hell are dealers going to do with

A mid-1970s 3-litre saloon on modern alloy wheels has lost none of its appeal in modern times, despite several years of improvements and development with the latest range of cars.

146

all the leftover 2500 and 2800s. When you hear of a 'special' like this – a car that once sold, in a slightly different form, for over $1,000 more – you suspect that somewhere there is going to be evidence of short-changing.

Upon the introduction of the Bavaria, the 2500 was discontinued in the American market, although it and the regular 2800 were still available in Europe, Britain and elsewhere. While journalists and owners acknowledged the Bavaria as a superb driving machine, there was something of an aura of dissent over the company's marketing policy. As a driving machine this car was close to perfection.

All that Glitters . . .

The engine was among the best, the car braked powerfully, handled predictably and was possessed of high levels of grip in fast corners. The interior was comfortable, mechanical noise minimal and build quality was well above the norm. But the US's official BMW importer, Hoffmann Motors, came in for some stick, and not for the first time. Max Hoffmann was a clever entrepreneur, who had introduced German cars to the Americans in the early 1950s.

He had 'dabbled' in them all including Volkswagens, Mercedes-Benz and Porsche. The BMW Bavaria was promoted as a luxury car at an interesting, budget price. In reality the cars were actually supplied with what *Road & Track* described as 'mandatory options', which automatically bumped up the purchase price.

Road & Track commented:

So the Bavaria's price isn't quite as low as it seems. Options brought our test car up to $6,386 including the $100 preparation charge, and it will be very difficult for any

customer to actually get a Bavaria without most of these options – particularly the air-conditioning, power steering, XAS tires, tinted glass and Skai upholstery. These items are more or less normal for a car of this type, and a basic Mercedes 250 Sedan costs over $6500. So, though the Bavaria's price is quite in line, it should not be considered a $5000 car. $6000 would be more like it.

This was valid criticism but largely ignored by customers. They certainly grumbled but wrote out cheques just the same, and the reasons were quite simple. The 2800 was one of the world's best and most exciting new sports saloons.

PROFITABLE STRUGGLE

By the early 1970s the motoring world had been truly gripped by BMW fever. During 1972 the Bavarian concern was producing 800 cars every day. Daimler-Benz made double this amount. But BMW were struggling to meet demand. During April 1972 David Blackburn's British concessionnaires sold almost 900 6-cylinder cars alone, despite an outstandingly high purchase price in Britain due to government-imposed taxes.

In 1971 the 2500/2800 range was added to in the guise of the quite formidable 3.0S and Si. This was a wholly logical progression, since the big saloon was merely to adopt the coupé's revised power unit. There were few who didn't rave about it. Apart from the 3.0 badge on the rump, these cars were outwardly indistinguishable from the two smaller-engined models. In Britian the 3.0 four-door saloon retailed at £3,999, which was expensive, but appeared to provide exceptional value for money by comparison with the 3.0CS coupé at £5,699.

Outwardly similar, the 5 series was developed from the first-generation cars and dubbed the 'world's best all-round saloon' by many journalists in the 1980s and 1990s.

The engine, with its familar 89mmx80mm bore and stroke opened the capacity out to 2985cc. With a compression ratio of 9.5:1 and Bosch fuel injection, maximum power of 200bhp was developed at 5,500rpm. The 4-speed manual transmission had the following ratios; First 3.85:1, Second 2.2:1, Third 1.4:1, Fourth 1:1, Final-drive ratio 3.45:1. The coupé's final-drive was slightly higher at 3.25:1.

For such a heavy saloon the 3.0 was blindingly fast through the gears. In *Autosport's* June 1972 test maximum speeds in each gear proved to be as follows: First 34mph, Second 62mph, Third 93mph. Top speed was a mighty 132mph.

This car didn't have the stunning looks of its coupé sister but, where performance is concerned, there was little to choose between the two cars. *Autosport's* John Bolster again failed to find serious fault with this grand 3-litre saloon and remarked:

> The Si saloon is a marvellous car to drive, being perfectly content to potter by the hour in London traffic but having immense performance on the open road.

As ever, the exhaust note was that of a classic, growling straight-six. Few cylinder configurations equal that unique sound. Flat-out acceleration tests revealed that it took no longer then 7.5sec to reach 60mph from rest, which was clearly quicker than a good many pukka sports cars of the day. But, as the passage of time has revealed, the biggest difference between the Munich saloon and a good many sports cars is that the BMW was capable of producing the same performance year after year, even when 'starship' mileage had been recorded on the odometer.

John Bolster was in the lucky position of having had the opportunity to test both the saloon and coupé on the same day, and could, therefore, make an accurate comparison between the two cars. He wrote:

> The Si accelerates rapidly to 132mph, which is the maximum speed claimed by the makers, at which the rev counter has just entered the red sector. The ignition cutout operates at about 133mph, which discourages further excursions into forbidden territory.

Bolster found the acceleration capabilities of the saloon and coupé almost identical save that the saloon, being slightly lower geared, felt livelier in the middle ranges.

With ZF worm-and-roller power-assisted steering, servo-assisted vented disc brakes all round, first-class ergonomics and a long waiting list at dealers' showrooms, these big saloons proved themselves to be as capable as any of their generation. Despite generally accepted wisdom, they also had lasting charisma. It is easy for devotees of Ferrari to describe the BMW's styling as Germanically bland, but for those who understand German stylists and the manner in which they think, these cars were exceptionally beautiful.

The 3.0 saloon remains one of BMW's most important models, but for reasons that hadn't become fully apparent until the 1990s.

6 BMW in Motor Sport: Old Faithfuls, Young Hopefuls

AN OLD TRADITION

BMW has a long and distinguished history in the world of motor sport, both on two and four wheels. In the hands of privateers and official works pilots, the machines from Bavaria have collected pots, points, and championships by the barrowload. Serious activity on the world's racing circuits has long been an integral part of the company's make-up, and for a few fundamental reasons.

The first and most important of these is that constructing a car for the purpose of competing at high speed against machinery from other manufacturers is exciting. It provides the human spirit with the kind of 'voltage' that can't be found in any other form of 'recreation', with the possible exception of building special aircraft for the same purpose.

To the true motor racing enthusiast, the ultimate test of human patience is spectating at an English cricket match, a game in which the maximum speed attained by any one player rarely gets much above 22mph – the very antithesis of the racer's *raison d'être*. Then, there are many other sports, like football, hockey, rugby, snooker, golf, tennis and squash. These all require the exercise of great human skill in some form or another, but for the racer they are of little interest.

Racing people are driven by the desire to experience the delights of speed – speed for its own sake – and by the sight and sound of a powerful thoroughbred on 'full song'. Racing cars are beautiful, make one hell of a racket, smell wonderfully of burnt oil and fuel and can also be dangerous. All of this is part of motor racing's great allure, and why BMW go racing. It is interesting that all of the truly great racers have one thing in common; contrary to popular belief it is not a desire to stash large quantities of prize money in a bank account. It is simply that they have to race.

Hans-Joachim Stuck, who drove for BMW during the 1970s before going on to score countless important victories as a works Porsche driver, once told this author that he had to go on racing. 'I just have to drive as fast as I can,' he remarked enthusiastically. 'There is nothing in the world to compare with the feeling you get when you complete a near perfect lap of the Nürburgring or Le Mans.'

There are one or two other reasons why BMW go racing. When one of the company's cars is successful in either a major or minor event, journalists devote many valuable column centimetres about such success in magazines and journals around the world. This gives BMW free advertising, and free publicity helps to sell cars, which is why BMW are in business. The other reason for

BMW have been successful in motor sport since the 1930s, and are as much a part of the modern historic scene as traditional sports machinery from Britain and Italy.

For many the pre-War 328 (seen here at Prescott Hillclimb) is the ultimate sports racing car, but the Munich company's real glory days lay well ahead.

going racing is that lessons learned on the track can be fed directly back to the engineers and designers with a view to improving both the racing and road cars.

There are few better ways of testing components – to destruction in some cases – than in the highly stressed engineering environment of a racing car. Of course, there are lots of cases of 'little old ladies' (and men), who have baffled manufacturers and road testers, by reducing a perfectly good car to a pile of rubble within just a few weeks of it leaving the factory. Professional testers have tried, in many cases, quite intentionally, to abuse a component in testing, and it has often withstood the strain. But these continue to break in the hands of the public.

What the professionals have rarely realized is, though, that there are certain sectors of the car-buying public who have little, or no, mechanical sympathy. There are some who, for example, select a gear for the day, and systematically subject their vehicles to an audibly premature death, but this is another story for another day.

EARLY DAYS

BMW's early successes between the two Wars included a team prize with three Dixis on the tough 1929 Alpine Rally, and victory in the 2-litre class in the Berlin–Spain–Berlin Rally of 1931 with a 3/15. In the last 24-Hour race at Le Mans before the outbreak of the Second World War, a 328 two-seater driven by Wensche/von Schaumburg-Lippe finished fifth overall and won the 2-litre class.

The 2002 and its closely related sister the 2000 provided the basis for development during the late 1960s. These cars remain popular in classic club race meetings today.

Apart from the works cars, the 2002s were prepared privately by the successful Schnitzer team, and others. Aerodynamic 'appendages' became wilder and wilder.

This marked a turning point and gave BMW the impetus for an all-out assault on the Mille Miglia in 1940. A team of five 328s developing around 140bhp apiece was entered to do battle with entries from Alfa-Romeo, Delage, Lancia and Fiat. The lightweight, aerodynamically styled bodies proved to be a critical factor for the BMWs in this event, as did meticulous preparation. *Motor Sport* noted the team's 'typical German care of detail', which can't have done much for morale among the members of Britain's sporting 'Dad's Army'.

Three of the team cars were open sports models, and two were closed coupés capable of a top speed in excess of 130mph. The 927-mile route of the 1940 event comprised nine laps of a 103-mile circuit and differed from previous Mille Miglias. This was due to the death of seven children in the 1938 event, and the new arrangement was part of an initiative to improve safety.

At the start Huschke von Hanstein took one of the closed coupés immediately into the lead, and drove the whole distance, apart from one lap when his co-driver, Walter Baumer, did a stint. Von Hanstein's fastest circuit was on his third lap. He averaged an utterly astonishing 108.8mph! Of 88 starters just 33 cars finished this truly gruelling event, and even von Hanstein had to slow down in the latter stages to conserve his BMW and prevent it from self-destruction.

Von Hanstein's victorious car had taken 8 hours 54 minutes and 46 seconds to complete the course, and had averaged 104.2mph. An Alfa finished second more than 16 minutes adrift, and the Brudes/ Roese BMW was placed third. Along with the Targa Florio, the Mille Miglia was one of the world's greatest and most punishing motoring competitions.

Finishing the Mille Miglia course was difficult enough, and winning was special

The glorious 3.CS provided the base car for BMW to go motor racing in the 1970s.

but, as Dr Mike Lawrence points out in his book *The Mille Miglia* (B.T. Batsford Ltd), the years following this great BMW victory would not look so rosy. Lawrence commented:

> Not so appropriate was the fact that on his overalls von Hanstein wore the insignia of the Waffen SS, an outfit which was to help ensure that the Mille Miglia would not be run again for some little time.

This effort in the 1940 event by BMW, demonstrated perfectly what the old company was capable of in top-line motor sport, but it would be a good few years before the motor sport division was in a position to build a racer again.

RECOVERY TAKES TIME

The first official post-War works racing cars were 'souped-up' 700 models. These took part in a variety of races – mostly on the European continent – and they notched up several class wins in both national and international events. It was largely thanks to Alex von Falkenhausen that BMW's racing activities were resumed. Von Falkenhausen was a racer who loved fast cars and powerful engines and, having placed Paul Rosche in charge of the engines division, BMW really started going places on the European circuit.

Von Falkenhausen was also something of a driving-talent spotter, and at one stage managed to secure the services of the

Belgian ace Jacky Ickx who, during the 1970s and 1980s, would go on to prove himself as the world's best all-round driver of all time.

SALOONS COME FIRST

The long slog to the top of the Formula One tree started with a 1,499cc 4-cylinder engine designed for the 1500 saloon in 1962. In production form this beautifully balanced and wonderfully strong unit developed 80bhp, and was eminently tunable for more power.

In 1963 the 1800TI saloon provided the basis for the first of BMW's homologated racing cars. Under international sporting rules in force at that time, a minimum of 200 racing versions were required to be built to qualify for homologation. It was this car that brought BMW to the attention of racing car enthusiasts – ordinary members of the public – with money to spend on BMW road cars.

During the 1960s saloon car racing fell into two distinct categories, and was nationalistic in its make-up. In Britain Colin Chapman's Lotus-Cortinas ruled the roost against BMC Minis, Jaguars and sundry American cars like the Ford Galaxy and Fairlane. The Cortina's position was ultimately toppled by Alan Mann's all-conquering Ford Escorts from 1968, and it was these cars that gave British spectators some of the most exciting and closest races in the history of the sport.

In Europe the Italians raced Alfa-Romeos, Fiats and Ferraris, while the Germans 'pedalled' away in their Mercs, Porsches and BMWs. Towards the end of the 1960s, saloon car racing became more international, with British, Italian and German manufacturers battling against each other at an ever wider variety of venues.

When Hubert Hahne won the 1964 German Saloon Car Championship in the 1800 TI-SA (*Sonder Ausführung*, or extraordinary sporting special), having scored a clutch of class wins throughout the year,

When driven by Quester and Hezemans, the works-entered CSLs were almost unbeatable . . .

. . . but the German Alpina threat could never be ignored. The Tourist Trophy at Silverstone in 1973 provided spectators with one of the closest battles in motor racing history.

Later to be associated with Jaguar's assault on Le Mans, Scotsman Tom Walkinshaw hotly pursues the Finotto / Facetti Alpina-built Group 2 CSL at Brands Hatch.

BMW's sporting image was assured. The jewel in the 1964 crown, however, was victory in the 24 Hour race at Spa in Belgium, and it didn't fall to BMW. The race was won by Rauno Alltonen in a Mercedes-Benz 300SE, after an 18-hour battle with Hahne's BMW, which was eventually placed second.

Far from being dispirited, though, the factory's people returned to Munich with a 'must-try-harder' attitude. Gerald Langlois and Pascal Ickx were engaged for the 1965 event and won! And kept winning this event in a monotonous fashion for many years. The space devoted in the international press to the Ickx/Langlois victory did not hurt BMW's bank balance one bit.

This racing onslaught continued for the next couple of years with the rapid 2000TI. When the 2002 arrived it took over from the older style model, and won the European Touring Car Championship in both 1968 and 1969 in Dieter Quester's skilled hands. Quester, of course, was von Falkenhausen's son-in-law, and would go on to make a name for himself in various racing formulae.

BMWs also enjoyed some success in rallying during the 1960s, mostly in the hands of rich privateers. The 2002 was particularly adept on both loose and tarmac surfaces, and although it was as fast as the Ford Escorts (until the advent of the latter's twin-cam engine), the Ford was considerably cheaper to run and simpler to service. These were two good reasons why the Ford product became the most successful ever car in rallysport and the BMW did not.

IN THE ROUGH

Towards the end of 1972 BMW scored its first big win in international rallying. The occasion was the sixth TAP Rally in Portugal, an event held in unseasonally wet weather. BMW fielded a 2002 Tii against seriously tough competition. In this era there was arguably a bigger variety of works teams than at any other period during the history of the sport.

All were serious about winning and spent hugely on resources to ensure this possibility. Citroën, for example, fielded specially built short-wheelbase versions of the DS21 and exotic Maserati-engined SM, employing the proven talents of such luminaries as Bjorn Waldegard to drive for the company. Renault had its fabulous all-conquering A110s, one example of which for this event was driven by Jean-Pierre Nicholas and Jean Todt, who led for much of the rally. Jean Todt, of course, would go on to achieve international fame in the 1990s as the leader of Michael Schumacher's attack on the Formula One Championship for Ferrari.

There were Triumph Dolomite Sprints and Ford Escorts from Britain, Porsches from Germany, Fiats from Italy, Datsun 240Zs from Japan and Dafs from Holland – a truly international flavour for the TAP Rally.

BMW's single factory-prepared 2002 Tii was driven by Achim Warmbold, a rookie on the TAP Rally. Tony Fall had used the same car on the Austrian rally, its engine developing around 190bhp. In Monte-Carlo fashion, the rally had various starting points, and eventually converged on the small town of Branganca in the north of Portugal.

A tough rally, and one in which tyre choice was critical, there were several casualties. Waldegard's SM Citroën, for example, suffered an oilpipe failure in the hydraulic system, which left him without brakes, power steering and suspension, and Warmbold's BMW suffered from a sticking throttle during the first day.

Darniche's Alpine Renault headed the leader board after day one with the BMW in

Despite the excitement produced by these cars and their great success, the championship virtually fizzled out in the aftermath of the 1973 oil crisis.

a close second place. Day two was also packed with incidents. A privately entered BMW driven by Asterhag failed to stop at the end of a stage and disappeared into a crowd of spectators, knocking two people over, and damaging the front MacPherson struts in the process. This car would later retire with complete suspension failure.

Warmbold's BMW ran like clockwork, and despite the treacherously slippy conditions and rough road surfaces, its driver made the most of the tremendous horsepower available under his right foot. Ingvar Carlsson's privately entered BMW had a piece of bad luck, when a backplate on a rear brake drum broke loose from the suspension arm, resulting in the car crashing hard into a wall. Warmbold was not without problems either. On one especially rough section the car rode over a large rock, which ripped open part of the floor on the passenger's side. Anders Gutlberg, driving one of the

Swedish entered BMWs, also dropped by the wayside with rear suspension failure.

John Davenport, who competed in this event and subsequently wrote a report for *Autosport* commented that, after Gutlberg's retirement, the Swede 'had to catch a train back to Lisbon, which took longer to get there than the rally'.

BMWs weren't the only retirements caused by serious mechanical breakages. Davenport reported:

On the second passage over Freita which was the only stage it rained during the night, Chenevière retired his Porsche and the Luybregts brothers broke a silent bush mounting on their Daf's transmission and had to stop and change it themselves. Caramulo the second time was terribly rough and claimed Smania, who broke his Fiat's differential and Ramaozinho who had been coming up quite nicely in the Citroën.

Borges also retired here when his engine started to seize and rather than destroy it completely, he decided to stop.

The rally took a very heavy toll. Thick fog close to the end of the event saw Bjorn Waldegard taking the Citroën for a trip across the scenery but, according to John Davenport, Warmbold demonstrated his superiority by setting the fastest time, and actually passed the second fastest car – Darniche's Alpine A110 – on the final stage!

This was a fine victory for BMW, and one which gave the company a great deal of free and welcome publicity in the international press. The TAP rally was an event devoid of political wranglings; there were no protests from teams about 'irregularities', infringements of rules and regulations, and none of the nonsense that was to characterize so many branches of motor sport in the years ahead. This was a good clean fight on rough roads, often in foul weather conditions, and BMW had not only survived, but had fought off fiercely competitive rivals to win one of the world's toughest events.

COMING OUT

By the end of the 1960s, BMWs were established winners and the roadgoing saloons were perceived by an increasingly enthusiastic public as the best of European sporting carriages. Independent tuning specialists like Alpina and Schnitzer took great interest in the cars, and not only raced them as private entrants, but began to manufacture all manner of tuning 'goodies' for the road cars. In fact, it was an Alpina-prepared 1600 that won the European Championship in 1970, during a period when the factory engineers were busy trying to perfect a new type of engine.

The quite remarkable 'Gosser Beer' CSL, which won the European Touring Car Championship in 1977 with Dieter Quester at the wheel, and in 1979 driven by Carlo Facetti and Martini Finotto.

FORCING A POINT

During the 1920s and 1930s, American, French, British, German and Italian manufacturers, had all built and fitted superchargers to their racing cars as a relatively uncomplicated route to gaining huge quantities of extra engine performance. Daimler-Benz, Bugatti and Alfa-Romeo had all flogged the 'blower' path, as had Sir 'Tim' Birkin with the big 4.5-litre Bentleys at the end of the 1920s. W.O. Bentley had never approved of superchargers, as they had two major drawbacks. They sapped engine power, as it was the engine that actually propelled their moving parts, and also consumed extraordinarily large quantities of fuel. The post-War Alfa Romeo Alfetta Grand Prix cars, for example, with their blown 1.5-litre straight-eight engines, were reputed to be capable of little more than 1.5mpg.

Although the car was hugely successful it needed a large fuel tank in the tail, and was endowed with variable handling characteristics as the fuel load lightened during the course of a Grand Prix.

There was, however, an alternative to supercharging, that was just as effective at producing more power, but without the disadvantages. This was the turbocharger, a device that utilizes spent exhaust gases to pressurize the fuel/air mixture. Turbochargers had been used on several aircraft engines before and during the Second World War but, by the 1960s had largely been forgotten about. With its huge and successful aero-engine background behind it, BMW had not quite forgotten about this form of forced induction and Alex von Falkenhausen resurrected the idea in 1968.

The famous CSLs can still be seen today at historic events, and are highly prized collector's items.

Has anyone ever made a better-looking or more purposeful sports racer than a CSL?

IN WITH A BANG

BMW's first turbocharged car engine was not a success, although the car it propelled was exceptionally fast. Producing around 270bhp at 7,200rpm the turbo BMW debuted at Snetterton, England, in 1969, led the race for a while and then detonated spectacularly. The engine was subsequently shown to be inadequate for coping with sudden and powerful boosts from the turbocharger.

This problem BMW took on board very quickly, learned a valuable lesson, and won the 1969 Saloon Championship. It was this experience that gave the company sufficient confidence by 1973 to launch the roadgoing turbocharged 2002 but, as noted elsewhere, the oil crisis killed this wonderful vehicle off very quickly indeed.

By the end of the 1960s BMW had proved its engineering and marketing capabilities beyond doubt, and by the time the motor sport department was formed as a separate division of the company in the early 1970s, many were pushed to remember that this was the same outfit that had faced bankruptcy and produced Isetta 'bubble' cars just a few years previously.

SALOON DOLDRUMS

At the beginning of the 1970s saloon car racing became something of a sad joke. In Britain, standard Ford Escort Mexicos were competing against Fiat 500s, wallowing American machines and even a Rolls-Royce Silver Shadow in one event. There were people with full competition licences who rented mundane Hillman Avenger saloons for the weekend, raced them on a Sunday, and returned them to the hire company on a Monday morning.

No doubt the drivers had their money's worth and a lot of fun, but these were not the kind of cars paying spectators particularly wanted to watch. In the British Saloon Car Championship there were four classes, and a mixed bag of entrants, with Chevrolet Camaros and Ford Mustangs at the top, Minis and Ford Escorts at the bottom, and Gerry Birrell's German-built Ford Capri RS2600 giving everyone something to think about from time to time.

In the European Championship there was a greater variety of machinery, and the lure of exciting driver's circuits, such as Spa-Francorchamps, the Nürburgring and the road track at Brno in Czechoslovakia. There were eight rounds in this Championship, which was won by Dieter Glemser in a Ford Capri, although Alfa Romeo won the manufacturer's title.

The best season-long battles, though, occurred between the Cologne-built Ford Capris and the heavy BMW 2500 and 2800 saloons. These BMWs were fine motor cars, but on the heavy side for serious saloon car racing. Despite the considerable efforts of Dieter Quester for BMW, the Fords of Dieter Glemser and Spaniard Alex Soler-Roig came out on top. Alfas cleaned up in the lower classes, although not without a fight from the aptly named Prince Fierfried von Hohenzollern, who all season drove his 2002 like a man possessed.

The big event of the 1971 season was the round at Paul Ricard in France, a 'double-six hour', that attracted top names including Jacky Ickx, Graham Hill and John Surtees. Despite the presence of these talents, it was the usual pairing of Glenser and Soler-Roig who won the day. Ford were having it all their own way, both in rallying and circuit racing.

SINGLE-SEATERS

A Ford badge also appeared prominently on the 'camboxes' of the Keith Duckworth-designed Cosworth V8 double-four valve engine, that was powering contemporary Grand Prix machinery to victory in virtually every race of each season.

After the heady days of the CSL, many tuners turned to the 3 series cars for competing in various European championships.

During 1970 BMW entered the Formula 2 fray with a 2-litre engine, that would snatch victory away from the Cosworth-engined cars in four rounds of the Championship, but this wasn't good enough for BMW. Rather than sitting on its corporate backside and patting itself on the back for gaining these spoils, the boys in Munich set about a proper assault on Ford's efforts.

By 1972 the company had secured the invaluable services of two experienced Ford men, Jochen Neerpasch and Martin Braungart. This formidable pair had been responsible for many Ford victories in major championship races and, from 1972, were charged with the responsibility of making the big 6-cylinder coupé work properly as a racing car.

BACK TO TOURING CARS

Hitherto BMW had gained a great deal of invaluable experience in racing saloons with the 'tiddly' 2-litre 4-cylinder engines, but the big sixes were a different ballgame altogether. It had been discovered that, at high speed, the standard bodywork of the lightweight 3.0CSL gave odd handling characteristics and a degree of instability.

This is precisely why the appendages – deep chin spoiler, huge rear wing, aerofoil on the trailing edge of the roof and small upright fins on the front wings – were developed for racing from the middle of 1973. In various guises these cars were all-conquering, and by 1974 other manufacturers lost interest and packed up in disgust.

PUKKA RACERS

The 3.0CSL provided BMW with a sound basis from which the company could develop the full-blooded racers. Apart from the factory-built cars, private teams were fielded by well-known tuning specialists like Alpina, who had been breathing on roadgoing BMWs for many years; the specification of the cars was, in some areas, only limited by the loose regulations in force at that time.

Bodywork modifications were even more radical than the roadgoing 'Batmobile's'; invariably the cars had large, boxy chin spoilers containing deep air scoops for cooling the brakes, vast wheelarch extensions to accommodate wide-diameter wheels, and a variety of wing shapes at the rear. The roof spoiler was similar to the Batmobile's, and the doors and front and rear lids were from the standard production car.

Modifications under the skin – relocation of the engine was not allowed – were subject to a minimum of 100 identical items being made. This latter rule was inaugurated to prevent the production of prototype specials, although in effect this is what BMW had accomplished, except, in contrast to pure prototypes, there were lots of them.

It's Still a BMW

Despite the adoption of aerodynamic wings, massively wide wheelarches – the rears had ducting for directing air to the engine, gearbox oil cooler and final-drive unit – and some pretty whacky paint schemes (one was painted by the late Andy Warhol), one of the most important aspects of these cars was that they were still recognizable as BMWs.

Dual headlamps, the kidney radiator grille, and BMW roundel on the panel in front of the bonnet were all retained. These were essential, of course, in BMW's marketing strategy. Inside the car the cabin was stripped of all passenger seating but, in many cases, retained the luxury interior panelling of the standard road cars. The

dashboard was redesigned to save weight, and to give improved access to the wiring in front of it – an essential safety feature.

The large-diameter stock steering wheel was changed for a small-diameter sports item, usually trimmed in leather with three 'drilled' spokes. Naturally, these cars were without carpeting, trim and a central console; in true racing fashion the gear lever was not shrouded with a rubber gaiter, and looked all the more purposeful for this.

A full rollcage that included side-impact beams across the doors, was installed, and welded directly to the bodyshell to give much enhanced torsional rigidity. The driver's seat was a traditional, lightweight racing item fitted with a four-point safety harness.

Under the rear lid, the space more normally occupied by the spare wheel and a piece of carpeting was packed the special racing equipment. Towards the rear was the oil tank for the dry-sump lubrication system, a brake fluid pump and the all-important fire extinguisher. A 32-gallon safety fuel tank was installed in the centre, and this had dual fillers that, for speed of operation, protruded through the top of the bootlid.

At the front of this 'luggage' compartment was the control unit for the anti-lock braking system – BMW were among the first manufacturers to fit ABS to a racing machine – twin electric fuel pumps, an alternator and the 12-volt battery. This was high-tech equipment in an age when an average family saloon had yet to be fitted with a stereo radio/cassette player as standard.

Apart from the boot being a convenient place in which to install all this equipment, the extra weight in the rear not only helped to counterbalance the weight of the engine, making for improved roadholding, but also greatly aided traction. This was always at a premium in the lower two gears.

Weight Watchers

Naturally, the suspension was heavily modified, much of this work having been directed by the ex-Ford man, Jochen Neerpasch. At the front the standard steel MacPherson struts were removed and replaced by aluminium-alloy struts with an attached magnesium-alloy hub carier. Each new strut saved 6lb in weight, while the hub carrier saved a further 8lb, and this had the important effect of reducing unsprung weight. This was intelligent thinking by engineers rather than amateurs.

Down the years, many thousands of well-meaning 'clubbie' racers have appreciated that weight has always been the principal enemy of speed. Taking a 'cooking' road car, many were easily able to shed weight by replacing the steel body panels with fibre-glass, or alloy, items, by stripping out the interior, removing the bumpers and all the other usual tricks.

This was all well and good, but had one major drawback. In the 1950s *Motor Sport's*

Denis Jenkinson embarked upon a weight-shedding programme with his standard roadgoing Porsche 356. By unbolting and removing unnecessary equipment, including the speedometer cable, the car was 168lb lighter than its normal overall weight of 1,876lb. Although this helped with acceleration, it upset the handling and balance of the car in quick corners, particularly on rough road surfaces.

In his book *Porsche Past and Present* (Gentry Books Ltd), Jenks explained:

The problem was an old one for sports cars, namely the unsprung weight to sprung weight ratio. All the weight came off the sprung part of the car, so that ride and suspension characteristics were not as good

Racing versions of the 3 series led to aerodynamic study becoming a serious science, and greatly benefited the road cars.

as in standard form. The extra performance gained by the reduction in weight aggravated the problem as well. What was needed was a reduction in the unsprung weight in direct proportion, with alloy wheels, alloy brake parts and lighter hubs and suspension members; the spring rates should have also been changed.

Jenkinson was a skilled engineer and knew his stuff, and what he and many others discovered during the 'dark' days of the 1950s, was that a racing car is a product of science – and a very expensive one.

The racing BMWs were very expensive! BMW had shed a relatively large quantity of weight from the front suspension, then, and had also increased the angle of the struts to accommodate the wide wheels and tyres. The standard rubber-bushed suspension arms and tie rods were pivoted on spherical joints in the traditional racing manner. In place of the worm and roller steering box, these racing cars had rack-and-pinion steering, which again allowed for a slight reduction in weight and also gave the steering a much more direct and positive feel.

At the rear the suspension arms were drilled with holes for lightness and the main control arms strengthened. The springs and dampers of the standard cars were replaced by a Bilstein spring-cum-damper unit, which was fully adjustable for varying ride heights. Bilsteins were also used up front – these too were lighter in weight – and the springs at both ends were made from titanium, an exotic and expensive material that Porsche had previously used for its conrods in racing engnes.

Breaking with the Past

The all-round brake discs, which had aluminium-alloy centres, saved nearly 8lb over each of the standard items, and were made by the German company ATE. Radially ventilated there were finned alloy calipers and Ferodo pads. German Teldix anti-lock brakes were in their infancy, of course, but had huge advantages in racing applications.

At one time, braking deeply into a bend had been considered the most heinous crime a racing driver could commit. The principals and teachers at schools of motor racing had preached for many years that a good racing driver got his braking finished with before entering a corner. Then, in the 1950s, Stirling Moss, who developed a technique of braking well into a bend, changed the way racers thought about driving.

Traditonally, the problem of braking in a corner was that it upset the balance of the car, particularly at high speeds. The inside front wheel developed a tendency to lock up, which would instantly throw the tail-end away from the straight and narrow, losing valuable time at best and causing a visit into the scenery at worst. Moss used this lack of balance to his advantage, although drivers of lesser skill continued to rely on traditonal techniques.

With the introduction of anti-lock brakes, the practice of dispensing with braking before entering a bend was virtually dead overnight. Electronics took care of the wheels, and prevented them from locking up almost anywhere on any circuit. This was a particularly valuable asset at challenging tracks like the Nürburgring in the Eifel Mountains of Germany.

Another advantage of anti-lock brakes was that they allowed for stiffer springs to be used, as they went a long way towards reducing a wheel's tendency to bounce after a loss of tyre adhesion. By preventing this loss of adhesion the car not only became more stable, but was easier on tyres, which meant fewer pit-stops for fresh rubber.

The 6 series BMW enjoyed a mixed bag of fortunes in the hands of privateers, but was never as successful as the CSLs.

Aluminium-alloy wheels were fitted, naturally, and these had split rims for varying the width of the wheels and tyres according to the requirements of different circuits.

Firing Order

Sitting behind the radiator 'nostrils' was a truly breathtaking power unit, loosely based on the production engine, but with more than double the latter's horsepower. Eventually, it developed 420bhp at 8,250rpm with a compression ratio of 11.2:1; this was normally aspirated engine technology at its ultimate.

Under racing regulations, it was essential to retain the production cylinder block (lowered in the chassis to reduce the centre of gravity and improve roadholding), and water pump. However, manufacturers were at liberty to modify virtually every other component, and BMW exploited this unusual freedom to full capacity.

With the bore increased to 94mm and the stroke kept at 84mm, the capacity was increased to 3,496cc. The same design of crankshaft was used and ran in seven main bearings, but was made from a finer grade of steel. Weight was shaved from the specially made and polished conrods, and even the bolts retaining the bearing caps were screwed into position (without nuts) to save weight.

Naturally, all reciprocating parts were perfectly balanced before assembly. Curiously, the high compression ratio was achieved with flat-topped pistons, a different route from several other manufacturers, who traditionally used domed items. The only big drawback with this 3.5-litre straight-six was that, with its cast-iron cylinder block, it was rather on the bulky and heavy side, which is why the company's racing department would eventually switch to four cylinders and turbocharging in future programmes.

Up until this time BMW had enjoyed mixed fortunes with its 4-cylinder Formula 2 engine. It wasn't a bad unit, which is why the cylinder head design was cribbed for the touring racers. Instead of a single-overhead camshaft, there were two camshafts. Instead of two valves per cylinder there were four, which improved the six's top-end 'breathing' ability enormously. Valve head diameters at 1.41in (inlet) and 1.19in (exhaust) were comparatively small.

Kugelfischer fuel injection, including a 6-piston pump similar in design to the one used by Daimler-Benz on the 300SL 'Gullwing' was fitted, and the intricate, tuned exhaust system exited the bodywork under the right-hand sill below the passenger door in an impressive brace of wide-bore pipes.

The engine drove the rear wheels (Heaven forbid that anything with a BMW badge should ever have front-wheel drive) through a 5-speed Getrag gearbox with synchromesh on all forward speeds. Synchromesh was something of a luxury on a racing machine, and its ease of operation was much appreciated by those who were lucky enough to have driven these cars.

A technical *tour de force*, these cars were explosively powerful, blindingly fast and had all but main rivals, Ford, scratching their heads in bewilderment. BMW had spent money – a lot of it – and had come up with a true world beater.

The mid-engined 6-cylinder M1 was a formidable road and racing car of the 1980s, and driven with success by such luminaries as F1 Champion Niki Lauda.

Popular on both sides of the Atlantic, the second-generation 3 series provided 'Clubbie' racers with the opportunity to go racing without spending a fortune on modifications.

On Track

Those who watched these cars in action will recall in every detail the manner in which they were conducted and the huge interest they caused. Glued to the tarmac, occasionally with a front wheel waving off the ground, the tail squatting hard on the ground, they were the spiritual successors to the mighty Porsche 917 sports racing cars of just a couple of years previously.

Big and brutal, yet refined, BMW brought a new class of competition to European and American racing circuits. During 1973 the battles with the RS Capris were epics. When the BMWs were driven by the likes of Hans-Joachim Stuck, Ronnie Peterson and Derek Bell, crowds flocked in their thousands to watch.

The 1973 TT race at Silverstone turned out to be a classic duel with close dicing throughout. The big Fords dropped out one by one, leaving the Bell/Ertl Alpina-entered CSL in the lead. But Dieter Quester was on a charge and catching the leader at a rapid pace when, with two laps to go, he ran out of fuel leaving Derek Bell and Harald Ertl with a well-earned victory, despite at one stage suffering a holed radiator.

Before this race Bell commented: 'It was a beautifully prepared car, and for some reason, I was fastest in the rain during practice. I just told them that I had been driving around quite quietly, but there I was, fastest.' Bell became a works driver temporarily after this showing.

Selected works drivers were rewarded for their efforts with a few choice perks, too.

Hans-Joachim Stuck, for example, was given a unique roadgoing version of the CS coupé fitted with a lusty V12 engine. But for the oil crisis of 1973, this unit might have found its way into the production cars, and been continued on the 6 Series that replaced the 3.0CS in 1976. Alas, it wouldn't see production until the advent of the 8 Series in the 1990s.

Championship Honours

The CSLs were also raced in 3.3-litre guise and developed 330bhp. A 3-litre version entered by Alpina won the opening race of the 1973 European season, and Ford the next two rounds, but BMW made up for this admirably at the Nürburgring with first and second placings – works entries – and third for an Alpina.

At the end of the 1973 season, BMW wound up with the Constructor's title in the European Championship, while the Dutch driver Toine Hezemans walked away with the Driver's Championship title. In 1974 the European Championship simply fizzled out; the effects of the oil crisis were being felt at all levels.

These cars were, however, raced in the United States during 1975, and proved particularly successful.

Posing as a Racing Driver

Not unnaturally, these cars were only ever entrusted to professional racing drivers and factory test drivers. Journalists didn't get a look in as a rule, which is why most of us can only imagine, difficult as it is, exactly what a pukka and powerful Batmobile was really like to drive.

The well-known American racing driver, Sam Posey, who had driven all manner of racing machines in his career, tested one

During the 1980s BMW were back in serious competition with a host of 3 series cars entered for the fast and furious German Touring Car Championship.

The amazing Dieter Quester was among the principal works drivers in the DTM.

of the track-prepared cars for *Road & Track* in November 1975, and his comments are well worth recording in some detail here.

Posey was flown to Kyalami in South Africa to evaluate and test the car in an attempt to discover whether or not it would be suitable for American IMSA racing. In charge of the test were team manager, Jochen Neerpasch, and chief engineer, Martin Braungart. Sam Posey, who had previously raced Ferraris commented:

To my great relief I found both of these gentlemen spoke perfect English. It had been one thing not to understand Italian when I was with Mr Chinetti's NART (North American Racing Team) team. The most technical discussions we ever had there concerned the proper choice of wine for dinner. With BMW I sensed things would be different.

This, if little else, highlighted the huge difference in approach to motor sport of two different nations. The German one in the new technological age would prove correct, as Ferrari's fortunes fell deeper and deeper into oblivion over the ensuing years.

Posey found the racing seat of the BMW uncharacteristically soft and well-padded, the rest of the interior stark and austere. He trickled the car out onto the track and completed two warming up laps before all hell let loose under his right foot ... eventually, at any rate. Even a driver of Posey's skill and judgement held a deal of respect for such a beast before exploring its outer limits.

Posey wrote:

Stepping on the throttle didn't seem as much a signal for the engine to produce power as it did a signal for the release of existing power. The reaction was so immediate and the power so sure, so positive, that it invited frequent use of the power-controlled slide.

Straight-line power he described as 'sensational'.

The anti-lock braking system, being entirely new to the world of the racing driver, was, at first, difficult to get used to. Posey, like most drivers of his generation, had been schooled in the traditional manner – slow into a corner, fast out of it. He commented:

Daimler-Benz provided BMW with the only serious competition.

I could drive remarkably deeply into turns before I braked. The problem was that my instincts weren't used to such deep braking, so at first the anti-lock braking system was only of marginal value to me.

Posey confessed that the following day he watched the Swedish genius, Ronnie Peterson (killed in a Lotus at the 1978 Italian Grand Prix), whose talents were second to none, drive the same car and learnt just how effective the anti-lock brakes could be, particularly in the wet. Peterson attacked the circuit in his customary smooth style, and passed one sports prototype after another.

Posey's criticism of the car included 'wrist-wrenching kickback' in the steering in certain difficult bends, which he concluded was probably the result of stiff sidewalls in the Dunlop tyres and too little caster. Despite the shortcomings of the Dunlops, they proved to be faster than the equivalent Goodyears.

After this session, Jochen Neerpasch reached the decision that the car was good enough for the IMSA series, and ran a team at the famous Daytona Speedway. Sam Posey was among the drivers. At Daytona the car's suspension was considerably softened up, and proved to be surprisingly unreceptive to changes in anti-roll bar settings. Despite a plethora of different types being made available, the transition from oversteering to understeering characteristics was almost entirely dictated by varying the ride height.

Posey Stuck with Hans

For the Sebring event Posey was paired with German, Hans-Joachim Stuck, a formidable driver in any formula, and Posey reckoned that he learnt a lot about the BMW from him. Stuck was undoubtedly the quickest and bravest of the BMW works drivers, and could perform the most extraordinary tricks in any make of car. Stuck had inherited a great deal of talent fron his famous father, who had driven, with a great deal of success, the fabulous Auto-Union Grand Prix cars before the War.

Hans-Joachim, though, had natural skill over and above anything his father had possessed and, being completely fearless, treated all of his racing cars with something approaching contempt.

Posey remarked:

Hans has been BMW's main driver during the entire development of the CSL and his confidence in the car enabled him to execute a maneuver which struck me as suicidal until I saw him get away with it over and over again. After the pits there are a pair of extremely fast left swerves. I had been backing off as I approached, then accelerating delicately, trying to keep the car from sliding. I was sure that if it did slide at such high speed I would lose control! But Hans neither backed off nor handled the car delicately. Instead he hurled the car at the turns and fought the wild slides with furious jabs at the wheel. Once I knew it could be done I tried it too, thereby discovering even when it is cocked sideways at 140mph the BMW can still be kept under control.

Stuck and Posey won the Sebring event with ease, which moved *Car & Driver* to comment: 'The era of Porsche domination in American GT competition is under serious attack – and may well be over.'

Although Sam Posey was undoubtedly a fine driver, his remarks above clearly demonstrated the huge gulf between someone like him and a true ace like Stuck. After further tests in Atlanta, where the team found even more speed through the corners after fitting wider wheels and tyres, the cars were entered for the race at Riverside. Posey and Stuck ran in separate cars.

Of this Posey commented;

For his car, Hans elected to stay with the limited-slip diff, while I opted for the locked rear because I thought I could control the car more precisely with the understeer. This decision, which turned out to be the wrong one, reflected the fact that I didn't think I could beat Hans at his own wild game. I was hoping I could make the car go faster by being tidier.

Impecunious privateers also benefited from the excellent power and handling package provided by the 3 series.

The third-generation 3 series upholds BMW honours in British and European Touring Car events.

This, Posey confessed, was entirely the wrong approach. The car, like any BMW, demanded to be torn limb from limb, kicked hard, blasted into the middle of the following week, and thoroughly abused to work properly for its keep.

As Posey remarked:

Characteristics like the steering kickback and the instability disguised the car's potential but did not limit it. In other words, try to drive the CSL smoothly and you can't do it, but go flat out, sliding at the most extreme slip angles and braking violently and all at once the car is totally alive, and surprisingly forgiving.

Naturally the car had been developed around, and to reflect, Hans Stuck's almost unique driving style, in the same way that Ferrari Grand Prix cars of the late 1990s were built around Michael Shumacher. The only way these machines could be driven properly was in the manner intended by the men who were responsible for their rare characteristics.

Needless to say, the Riverside event was won by Stuck, with Posey placed second. At all future events Posey threw all driving theories out of the window – the BMW and Stuck defied them all. Stuck's speed in a CSL was incomparable. There was simply no-one to touch him.

Sam Posey concluded:

At every race I've been a little closer to matching Hans' speed. Meanwhile, from a few car lengths back, I've been treated to the most hair-raising driving style I've seen yet, and over the years drivers like Parnelli Jones, James Hunt and Jody Schekter have shown me some pretty outrageous stuff. Following Hans, I've seen his car totally sideways in the turns, or oversteering off the track on the outside, or sliding through an apex, the inside wheel wrenched so far off the ground it was like the hoof of a horse pawing in the air.

BMW owners are rarely away from the race tracks, where 'hares' have always been welcome.

These were the truly 'golden days' of BMW's foray into the world of production sports/saloon car racing. These lightweight racing cars made a huge impact in all markets where BMWs were sold. Suddenly, by the mid-1970s BMW had become a real opposition force to Porsche – the car that all drivers aspired to.

From the mid-1970s, BMW's saloon car efforts went into decline until the debut of the M3 in the 1980s, when the Munich products came to the fore again. With the CSLs BMW had proved a point; they were capable of winning. The early 5 Series cars were raced in sundry British and European saloon car events, but not with the success of their illustrious forebears.

What began in the 1960s as a serious attempt to bring the name of BMW to public attention with saloon car racing progressed through the exciting days of the 1970s, and culminated in Nelson Piquet's Formula 1 Championship victory in the Brabham-BMW in 1983.

Since then the company has never looked back, has never been far away from the racetracks in some capacity or other, and looks poised for future success in the twenty-first century.

7 The 'Best Car in the World' – Made in Munich

CHANGING TIDES

In the early 1970s Rolls-Royce was heading for the first of its serious financial hiccoughs. The company's principal model was the Silver Shadow saloon, a car capable of conveying four adults in comfort and silence. Its 6.2-litre V8 engine was simple in construction, long-lived and capable of gracefully moving the car from rest to a leisurely top speed of 120mph.

With the aerodynamic properties of a Fordson tractor travelling in reverse gear, and the handling characteristics of an epileptic boar, these cars were not owned by the type of person who traditionally liked to get a move on.

Journalists who tested these cars waxed lyrical about the highly varnished veneer dashboards, the beauty and quality of the leather upholstery, sycophantic waves from traffic policemen, but rarely mentioned anything about the car's road manners. To be perfectly candid, the Silver Shadow, and so many of its successors, were expensive dinosaurs.

From a driver's point of view the 3.0 BMW saloon was a vastly superior machine, but cost substantially less to buy and run. These facts were not lost on the luxury market's potential customers. BMW were only too happy to oblige them, and have been doing so ever since.

When BMW introduced the 3.3L (3,295cc) with a 4in longer wheelbase in 1975, these handsome saloons were projected well into S Class Mercedes territory – and Rolls-Royce bumbled on. More than 56,000 3-litre and 3.3-litre cars were sold between 1971 and 1977, and there were in excess of 132,000 of the 2500/2800 saloons built between 1968 and 1977. These were healthy production figues that brought handsome profits.

This success was down to producing fine luxury saloons with mass-production techniques. The fine craftsmen and women at Rolls-Royce exercised fine skills long since forgotten elsewhere in the motor industry. Regrettably, these skills were no longer needed in the rough and tumble of the new age. A man at Crewe would spend many hours building a radiator grille by hand. The finished item was beautiful to behold.

Conversely, BMW had a machine capable of stamping out many radiator grilles in the same time that a Rolls-Royce craftsmen would take to complete just one. At this time, there were one or two gifted individuals at Rolls-Royce capable of painting a 'coachline' by hand, along the entire length of the Silver Shadow's bodywork. Such skills are rare, but this was in an age when 'coachlines' were not fashionable, and there were too few customers to appreciate the skill anyway. Ignoring the demands of the real world – and Rolls-Royce did – produces dire financial consequences, as BMW had discovered in the 1950s. BMW were on the up.

TAKE FIVE

By 1972 the ageing mid-range 2000 saloons had served their purpose and were put out to grass. With nearly 143,500 units having left the factory, the workforce waved goodbye to the car that had done so much to lift the company's fortunes. In its place came the first of the 5 Series cars. In time, and with development, the 5 Series would become the definitive four-door saloon of the late twentieth century.

The earliest incarnation was launched to coincide with the ill-fated 1972 Olympic Games held in Munich. Much publicity was to be gained by BMW from this ploy, but, unfortunately, the 1972 Olympics is remembered more for the cold-blooded murder of Israeli athletes by Arab gunmen. A gun battle at the Fürstenfeldbruck Airport, in which five guerrillas and a policemen were killed, brought the saga to an end.

This outrage naturally gained the attention of the world's media to such an extent that little else appeared in news reports for several days. And there were certainly few who noticed BMW's efforts to debut an important new saloon car. A mid-range vehicle styled very much along the lines of the 2500/2800/3.0 saloons, the Five's debut might have been untimely in one sense, but was opportune in another. It was an affordable, economical BMW that would ride the oil crisis of the following year, whereas the larger-engined cars took something of a sideways bang.

The magnificent 5 series was launched in 1972, and provided sumptuous transport for the well-heeled middle classes.

Made at the Glas Dingolfing factory, these were conventional cars made to BMW's remarkably high standards. The all-steel bodyshell was a four-door (two-door versions were never made), with rather conservative styling. BMW's deliberate policy of employing a large glass area was retained, as were the kidney-shaped grille, twin headlamps and distinctive rake of the radiator grille.

The Funfer, as it was known in Germany, laid down a style that BMW would develop long into the future. As the range was expanded and sales increased, it became apparent that BMW's cutomers had rather conservative tastes. From this point on radical changes in styling were never to be on the agenda.

Rugged, tough and reliable the 5 series became a popular alternative to the evergreen Peugeot 504 in African countries.

Comfortable, quick and with the well-established handling package, the Five (dubbed 520 at first), was intended for those elements of the middle class who aspired to Mercedes-Benz ownership. One senior member of BMW's management team once expressed genuine disbelief as to why anyone would want to own a Mercedes. 'How can people drive those trucks?' he asked.

Inside the Five there was a shrouded instrument binnacle, also a distinctive feature of interior design that would be retained in future models, with each gauge illuminated with orange characters. No other saloon car had such an unusual feature, and it made BMW owners feel a little bit more special. What the car lacked, though, was an engine capable of doing justice to such a powerful chassis.

At first a 2-litre 4-cylinder single overhead-camshaft unit, capable of producing a top speed of 110mph, was installed. It was to BMW's conventional design, and one of the finest in-line fours made anywhere, but had none of the 'autobahn-burner' image portrayed by the company's racing cars. The 520 was, however, marginally quicker than the 125bhp Volvo 144S 2-litre, which would nudge 105mph in favourable conditions. Saab and Volkswagen weren't in the same league during this period, which served to emphasize BMW's niche market.

The rest naturally follow

Within a year of the 4-cylinder 520's debut, the first of the 6-cylinder Fives arrived in the form of the 525 (2.5-litre). In 1974 the 'down-market' 518 came along with the 1.8-litre 4-cylnder engine. This was a relatively inexpensive and grossly underpowered car, clearly designed to make inroads into the upper end of the market occupied by range-topping Fords, Vauxhalls, Opels, Volkswagens, Fiats and so on.

The 528 and 530 (2.8 and 3-litre straight-six) models joined the range in 1978, both of which renewed the onslaught against Daimler-Benz with some considerable vigour. By this stage the two marque's products were not that different from each other.

As *Car & Driver*'s Patrick Bedard pointed out in 1975:

> In addition to certain obvious similarities between Mercedes and BMW cars – size and price being the most conspicuous – the two firms also share a common philosophical ground. Both are committed to building driver's cars rather than painless transportation passenger cars.

Bedard went on to remark that, whereas the Stuttgart concern celebrated its many motoring achievements with cars that felt as though they were carved out of granite, BMW's approach was to make finely tuned machines that 'encourage participation from their drivers and offer smooth and accurate response as a reward'.

Car & Driver made a rather odd comparison between the 530i and three rivals – the Cadillac Seville, Mercury Monarch and Volvo 242. In terms of accelerating and braking, the BMW knocked spots off these, but fared less well in interior sound level tests. Not surprisingly, the 2-litre 4-cylinder Volvo proved best on fuel consumption. The BMW also scored badly on purchase price.

With optional metallic paint, air-conditioning, manual sunroof and a radio, the car retailed in America at more than $11,000.

Available with a choice of 4- and 6-cylinder engines, the 5 series had elegant styling and provided sporting motorists with an exciting alternative to conservative saloons from Stuttgart.

In 165bhp 2.8-litre guise, the 528 was a rapid machine with exceptional road manners. By 1975 this car had established BMW as a builder of cars for successful people.

The Cadillac was less than $10,000 but, as *Car & Driver* commented:

> If you think the mass-production interior of a Granada Ghia looks more expensive . . . well, the Germans know it isn't . . . Further, they reckon that if you can be seduced by that kind of surface flash, you probably wouldn't know a driver's car from a passenger's anyway. And they're just independent enough to consider that's your problem anyway.

In 1974 BMW sold 15,000 cars in the United States, roughly equal to General Motors' daily output in 'boom' times, but it was the bespoke nature of the German product that ensured a continuous rise in sales. By the mid-1970s 4-cylinder and 6-cylinder cars were selling in roughly equal quantities. In 1976 the company steered itself in a new direction and took stock.

THE MODERN ERA

In 1976 BMW reached something of a 'watershed'. The company had made huge progress over 20 years or so, largely because of its unshakable belief in its products and marketing strategy. The people in Munich were in a happy financial position. A new range of cars had been in the planning stage for some time, and their launch ushered in a new era for BMW and its fortunes.

The '02 was replaced by the 'slinky' 3 series, the 6 series replaced the shapely Karmann-built 3.0CS, and in 1977 the 2500/2800/3.0 saloons were dropped in favour of the 7 Series. Production of the

BMW 530i (1972–79)

Layout and Chassis	Unitary construction, all-steel, four-door saloon

Engine

Type	In-line
Block material	Cast-iron with conventional water jackets
Head material	Light alloy
Cyinders	Six
Cooling	Water
Bore × stroke	89 × 80mm
Capacity	2,985cc
Valves	Two per cylinder
Timing	Single ohc
Compression ratio	8.1:1
Maximum power	176bhp (SAE) at 5,500rpm
Maximum torque	185lb ft at 4,500rpm
Fuel system	Bosch L-Jetronic fuel injection
Fuel tank capacity	18.5gal (84ltr)

Transmission

Gearbox	Synchromesh 4-speed manual
Ratios	First 3.86
	Second 2.20
	Third 1.40
	Fourth 1.00
	Final drive 3.64:1
Clutch	Single dry-plate

Suspension and steering

Front	Independent by MacPherson struts, coil springs and anti-roll bar
Rear	Independent by semi trailing arms, coil springs and anti-roll bar
Steering	Power-assisted recirculating ball with 3.5 turns from lock to lock
Tyres	Michelin XVS 195/70HR14 radial
Wheels	Pressed steel 14inx6in

Brakes	Power-assisted vented discs front and rear

Dimensions (in/mm)

Track	Front 56/1,422
	Rear 58/1,473
Wheelbase	104/2,637
Overall length	190/4,823
Overall width	67/1,707
Overall height	56/1,422
Dry weight	3,315lb (1,503kg)

Performance

Maximum speed	127mph (204km/h)
0–60mph (0–100km/h)	10.3sec
Standing quarter mile (0.4km)	17sec
Fuel consumption	17–22mpg (12.9–16.6ltr × 100km)

For details of other models in the 5-series range, see main text

5 Series was inevitably continued, and BMW cleverly started its policy of 'overlapping' engines between models. This not only cut production costs but greatly broadened choice.

Enthusiasts loyal to BMW heavily mourned the loss of the 2002 and the beautiful coupés – and still do – but their replacements were worthy successors, if not as striking in terms of styling. The new cars were genuinely improved. The 3 Series, for example, was the first production BMW to have rack-and-pinion steering instead of the old fashioned worm-and-roller units. This made the steering discernibly lighter and more positive and, having been re-geared, was much easier in use both at parking speeds and on the move.

The entire range – 3, 5, 6 and 7 series – was similarly styled to maintain what manufacturers now refer to as 'corporate image', a facet of design that would become ostensibly more important as the years ticked by. Generally, the new cars were bigger, heavier, more powerful and more expensive to buy than their predecessors.

When referring to the new cars, purists spoke in terms of 'blandness', 'clinical character' and 'flabbiness', but purists were in a minority. And those purists, who in recent times have embarked upon inevitably expensive and complex restorations of a 3.0CS coupé, for example, have also begun to see the point of the modern machines.

In the four models, there were engines ranging in size from the 1.6-litre 4-cylinder

A wolf in sheep's clothing the 1979 M535i was a thundering 155mph express, but an increasingly impractical one on the overcrowded roads of Europe.

units through to the 3-litre six, and eventually the 3.5-litre six. BMW also returned to making a 2-litre six that was available in both the 3 Series 320 and 5 Series 520 models. To a fresh design with redesigned combustion chambers, these units were, nonetheless, to the classic BMW overhead-camshaft format.

A 2-litre straight-six had been famously campaigned in the company's pre-War 328 – still one of the world's truly great cars – and enthusiasts lusted after the modern unit in ever increasing numbers. The 3 Series would eventually get 2.3 and 2.5-litre sixes, which would result in some of the most desirable driving machines ever. The well-known English racing driver, Barrie 'Whizzo' Williams, a man possessed of quite extraordinary driving skills and a great fan of BMWs, once remarked that he knew of no other car in the history of internal combustion that would live with a 325i.

This was praise indeed coming from a man who had driven a huge variety of fast road and racing cars in a successful career that spans several decades.

THE SAME, ONLY BETTER

All the cars made after 1976 stuck to a basically well tried and tested formula. There were MacPherson struts and coil springs up front, and semi-trailing arms and coil springs at the rear. The engines were eminently tunable, and specialists like Alpina had a field day – as did customers.

Of the first 3 series cars *Road & Track* commented:

The new small BMW is a logical step forward improving on what needed improving and leaving what was well enough alone. One might want for a more fascinating technical content in a new

model, but a driver is unlikely to wish for more car. The 320 or 320i, in which ever form the 3 Series is presented in North America, should help BMW of North America attain its sales goals for the next few years after it's launched in the summer of 1976.

The new cars were race-bred and it showed. The colossal fortune BMW had spent on motor racing had paid off and the road cars were hugely improved as a result. Even the 7 Series, the biggest and heaviest of post-War BMWs, handled and held the road like a dream. But there was considerably more to these cars than a luxuriously appointed interior, and the ability to cruise at high speed effortlessly between cities. They were also full of complexities.

The 7 Series, for example, had no fewer than 30 electric motors, if all extra-cost options were specified. In addition the 7 and 6 Series had a test button on the dashboard for checking the oil level in the sump, brake fluid and screen washer reservoir levels, wear in the brake pads, and health of the bulbs in the tail-lamp clusters. These were just some of the technical advantages gained as a result of the racing programme. It was the beginning of yet another technical revolution, and BMW were at the forefront, as the company continues to be.

In the 7 Series BMW had succeeded in making a voluminous and large car, that felt like a much smaller one from behind the wheel. What the stylists at this stage had not mastered, with either the 7 or 6 Series, was a large car that looked like a small one. This would come with the 850i coupé and second generation 7 Series. Major competitors were the Mercs and Jaguars but, with BMW's deliberate policy of going further up-market, much cheaper rivals like the Peugeot 604, Volvo 264 and aged Rover 3500 V8, didn't really get a look in.

For a luxury saloon at a premium price the 5 Series sold almost beyond BMW's wildest dreams. Up until 1981, almost three-quarters of a million of them had been 'knocked out', and sales began to escalate after this time, when the 'face-lifted' model was launched. Similar to the original Funfer, but with much leaner body styling, this model was quickly established as the doyen of high-performance saloons.

It was quick, stylish and beautifully executed. And it had caught Daimler-Benz out well and truly with its corporate trousers around its ankles. Mercs of this era were perceived to be beautifully engineered motor cars on the one hand, but rather stodgy gas-guzzlers on the other. The 5 series was for those who were really going places and, in the case of the M-powered 24-valve 3.5-litre car launched in the mid-1980s, rather quickly too.

Incorrectly dubbed as a wolf in sheep's clothing by some branches of the popular media, the M5 was capable of carrying four or five adults in comfort all the way to 155mph. Acceleration was brutal and exciting; 60mph from rest could be accomplished in 7sec. The same engine fitted to the 635CSi gave this model instant and lasting classic status.

A QUESTION OF BALANCE

BMW's marketing policy was as aggressive as the frontal appearance of the company's range. In publicity material BMW took an open swipe at some of its nearest rivals. They commented:

> To achieve the running characteristics and turbine-like smoothness typical of BMW's 6-cylinder in-line engines, the primary and secondary forces and the moment of inertia must be fully balanced – as is the case in a 6-cylinder in-line engine. In a V6 engine, on the other hand, only the primary forces are balanced, while with a 5-cylinder in-line engine there is no balance at all – neither of the primary nor secondary forces. As a result, both these arrangements have inherent disadvantages as far as smooth running is concerned.

This side-swipe at a V6 was aimed at the upper echelons of anything and everything made in France and Italy, whereas the little dig at the in-line 5-cylinder was, since no-one else had bothered with this innovative configuration, clearly spearheaded at Audi's quattro. By 1985 the quattro was showing a clean pair of heels to everything in the international rally circus, and whether a 5-cylinder engine was balanced or not, Ingolstadt's best was making good capital.

Interestingly, throughout the 1980s and 1990s, Audi has been one of BMWs closest rivals. However, despite the success of the rally quattros, Audi appears to have lost out in the marketing stakes, and the Ingolstadt concern has no-one to blame but themselves for this. Audi's rich and successful racing history started with the Auto-Union Grand Prix cars in the 1930s. It is a past that Audi have been slow to capitalize on, and while BMW were in the ascendance during the 1970s, Audi sat back and watched almost helplessly.

TACKLING PROBLEMS

In 1983 the Mk2 3 Series was launched. Larger than its predecessor, and with angular, more conservative styling, it came at a time when several manufacturers were boasting about their achievements in creating cars with low aerodynamic drag. The 3 Series was the staple diet of the

In 1982 the styling was made crisper, and sales of the 5 series increased by 30 per cent almost overnight.

range, to which an emergent class of people aspired.

Engines ranged from the 1.8-litre 4-cylinder to the 2.5-litre in-line 6-cylinder, with a special 145mph M3 version eventually being added. These cars were more economical than the ones they replaced, handled better, produced more power and were greatly desired by the Upwardly Mobile, or Yuppies as they became known.

As a result of this, BMW suddenly acquired an image problem, which was partially due to the company's own marketing ways. Jokes about Yuppies and their BMWs in almost every branch of the media began to tarnish BMW. 'Lager louts' owned BMWs. Porsche suffered in a similar way, except that the Stuttgart cars were associated with drug dealers instead.

History was repeating itself; Jaguars had been associated with bank managers and bank robbers alike during the 1960s; mud has a nasty habit of sticking for a very long time.

The 1980s threw up a host of other problems too. Apart from increasing competition from other manufacturers, there were problems of increased pollution from exhaust emissions. Germany's Green Party packed a great deal of political clout, and there was a pressing problem about the speeds at which BMWs were capable of travelling. Even the lowest-powered cars were capable of around 115mph. Along with a number of other German manufacturers, BMW agreed to limit their most powerful machines to a maximum speed of 155mph. Not to have done so was seen in Germany as irresponsible, although many, of course, still question the wisdom of being allowed to travel at 155mph.

One of the other pressing problems was fuel consumption. Powerful, large-capacity engines consume large quantities of fuel. BMW addressed this partially by reducing the weight of their bodyshells by 8 per cent. State-of-the-art laser welding techniques were employed to achieve this, but engine development played an equally important role.

By the 1980s BMW had also become involved in the diesel engine market. Such was the pace of technological progress, that the company's diesel power units were not only acknowledged as the world's smoothest and among the most economical but, in turbocharged form, were also the most powerful. By the late 1980s, though, the use of diesel fuel was beginning to be seriously questioned, as it was thought to pose a threat to human health. Particles of soot in exhaust emissions were thought to be capable of penetrating the human body's smallest cells, but there was no research to support this theory until the late 1990s.

These cars were made to be driven hard, and developed a legendary reputation for reliability.

Turbocharged diesel versions – not available in all markets – became a benchmark by which all other 'oil burners' would be judged.

This, combined with fears over harmful emissions from conventional petrol engines, despite the use of three-way catalytic converters, has seen BMW and others diversify on an experimental basis into the murky world of alternative fuels. The company has had a great deal of success with hydrogen powered engines, and some with battery 'fired' propulsion. The former may have a future, although not while there is a glut of oil readily available, while the latter, without a major technical breakthrough, appears to be one of the twentieth century's biggest motoring 'white elephants'.

It has been known for many years that there are plenty of alternative fuels to petrol and diesel; LPG and alcohol fuel distilled from sugar are but two, but a lack of political will holds these back.

INNOVATION AND PACE SETTING

By 1986 a revised 7 series was launched. An all-new 5 series came in 1988 and these were closely followed by the startling Z1 two-seater sports car and V12 850i, the latter to replace the largely unloved

6 Series. The Z1 was a particularly interesting car, as its galvanized chassis monocoque hull and epoxy resin foam floorpan, was clothed in a series of removable plastic panels.

With superlative performance, almost unrivalled handling properties, this 140mph rocket was a gamble that paid off for BMW. Sports cars weren't selling particularly well at this time, but there was no shortage of customers for this instant classic. The Z1 was followed by the even more startling Z3 in 1997. This was the company's first truly sporting machine since the 1930s, and did as much to satisfy the appetites of discerning enthusiasts as the 328 had done before it.

The big, handsome 850i coupé on the other hand, with its 5-litre V12 engine up front, was in an altogether different league. This was a new flagship and, despite the usual nonsense from some journalists that the car wasn't as good in some areas as it should have been, the 850i and closely related CSi sister, stand among the truly remarkable cars of the twentieth century.

Ferrari's production and racing cars had ensured that a certain mysticism had grown up around the classic V12 engine configuration. More cylinders meant more power, elephantine torque and the smoothest running. Apart from Ferrari, Lamborghini and Jaguar had also gone down the V12 route. But true to form BMW took V12 technology several steps further.

In the German tradition this engine was also reliable – good for very high mileage – and rarely needed expensive remedial work. As a result the 850i became one of the world's most respected Grand Tourers, appreciated by those who could afford the high purchase price, and eye-watering running costs.

When Grand Prix car designer, Gordon Murray embarked on the 'no-expense-spared' McLaren F1 'supercar' in the 1990s, this gifted innovator's brief was to create a car without compromise. In brief, it was to be the best road car ever made, a tall order for any mortal to deliver. The cars were to be sold with a price tag in excess of half a million pounds each – the racing versions even more – and anything less than perfection, down to the last nut and bolt, would have been inexcusable.

There was no shortage of power units available to Murray, but he chose the V12 BMW unit, as it gave more horsepower per litre than any other unit. Apart from this, Gordon Murray had enjoyed a good working relationship with BMW since their collaboration on the Formula One Championship-winning Brabham project in 1983. In 1995 a BMW-powered McLaren F1 claimed victory in the Le Mans 24-Hours – the ultimate prize for the ultimate car.

REFLECTIONS

The story of BMW's rise, fall and rise again, is one of the most extraordinary among many in the German motor industry. In contrast to the British motor industry, a large chunk of which is now owned by BMW, the Munich company has climbed admirably from the mire when the chips were down. Huge, almost unimaginable success, after being brought to the brink of bankruptcy in the late 1950s, can largely be attributed to the German capacity for solving, rather than giving up on, problems. This has been a national trait in various branches of German industry throughout the course of the twentieth century.

A perfect illustration as to how German mentality functions can be gained, not from the motor industry, but the German wine industry. Growing grapes and making wine from them can be a fun and lucrative pastime. However, Germany once had a problem; the country is too far north and too cold for grapes to ripen properly.

A grape variety was, therefore, required, that would ripen in the correct manner. If such a grape didn't exist, then there was the possibility of inventing one. Science would come to the rescue. German wine was consequently fermented to a virtually undrinkable acidity, added to unfermented grape juice and the result, pure and simple, was a delicious and distinctive fruit flavour for which the industry has become world famous.

Traditionally, a problem that arises in the German motor industry such as, for example, the need to decrease fuel consumption, is solved by people in this specialist field performing expensive research. The simplicity of the approach always gets results.

PRESENT AND FUTURE

In 1998 BMW continues with its latest generation of 3, 5, 7 and 8 series cars, with its policy of overlapping engines between models. They are all expensive, beautifully made cars that motoring enthusiasts regard as among the best to be found anywhere. The one-time aim of knocking Daimler-Benz off its pedestal hasn't happened – far from it – but BMW is established as one of the most respected car makers. Having acquired the Rover group in the mid-1990s, and made unprecedented changes to this company's structure, the latter's success remains almost on a knife edge.

Arguably the last of the classic BMW saloons, the 3.5-litre M5 would give way to a wholly new breed of cars, but 'drivers' didn't necessarily consider the later machines to be better.

A tussle with Volkswagen during 1998 to acquire Rolls-Royce, resulted in victory for the Wolfsburg concern, or at least, a partial victory. From 2002 – an appropriate year – BMW gains the right to use the Rolls-Royce name, while Volkswagen retains the right to the Bentley appellation.

Whatever the eventual outcome of this 'bed-fellow' arrangement, German car makers across the board have, through careful planning, poised themselves especially well to meet the considerable challenges – and there will be several – of the twenty-first century.

Index